MW00526497

IN SEARCH OF OUR IDENTITY

UNDERSTANDING BEHAVIOR IN BIPOLAR DISORDER

John McManamy

The Bipolar Expert Series

Published by mcman

For more information, visit bipolarexpertseries.com and
mcmanweb.com

© Copyright John McManamy, 2016, 2017. All rights reserved.

First paperback edition: Dec 2016
Revised with new content: June 2017

Book and cover design, Map of Reality and graphs by John McManamy.

Map of Reality and original images in this book © Copyright John McManamy, 2016. All rights reserved.

ISBN 978-0-9852394-9-7

To Jenefer Heartfire McCormick and Kelly Fitzpatrick, two amazing people with huge hearts who came through for me in a time of need.

CONTENTS

PREFACE

MY GOAL in this book is to help make you an expert patient. This is the second book in *The Bipolar Expert Patient Series*, and it starts off exactly the same as my first book, as will my next books. Here's the deal, which is an exact copy-and-paste:

Patients who take the lead in learning about their illness and in managing their own recovery fare far better than those who simply wait for something to happen. This applies across all chronic illnesses, not just bipolar disorder.

Okay, we're off the copy and paste. In my first book in this series, NOT JUST UP AND DOWN, I felt it necessary to set out at length my credentials as an expert patient. This included my lived experience with bipolar, my background as a financial journalist with a law degree, my involvement as an advocate, my accomplishments, and my many years researching and writing about my illness.

If I had an MD or a PhD to my name, there would have been no need for the big song and dance. But the expert patient movement is fairly new, and readers are justifiably skeptical. Back in 2005, I was fortunate enough to find an enlightened editor in Sarah Durand, and a year later HarperCollins published my book, *Living Well with Depression and Bipolar Disorder*. To my knowledge, with regard to my illness, this was an expert patient first. Until then, bipolar patient knowledge came wrapped in the mandatory memoir.

Nevertheless, I didn't stray too far outside the lines. But by the time I came to conceiving this series, I was ready to assert my authority. I would connect my own dots, form my own conclusions. "Scientific discovery and innovation is exploding at an exponential pace," I wrote in the last chapter to NOT JUST UP AND DOWN, "but we the patients represent the essential reality check. Always, always, we need to be talking—and talking back."

If this sounds self-evident to you, then thank you—we're making progress. This means I can keep my prefatory song and dance routine short. And maybe the one for my next book will even be shorter. Who knows? One day I may not even have to do one.

When that day comes, my job will be done.

Now for my black box warning: This is a book about behavior, not mood. That was the topic of my previous book. I have made a good faith effort to summarize some of the main points of that book, but I urge you to get you own copy. The two books are meant to be read together, in any order you like.

Likewise, this is not a book about recovery. That will be the focus of my next book in this series. Thus, no mention of the practical tips and tricks we can do to help manage some of our problematic thoughts and emotions we talk about here. Be patient—that book is on the way. In the meantime, bear in mind: Recovery is a complete nonstarter without understanding. The "bipolar expert" I refer to in this series is you. Always, always, we have to be our own experts.

With regard to behavior: Without a basic understanding of how we think and feel and get along with others, our depressions and anxieties and manias are going to make no sense at all to us. We will be reduced to blindly reacting rather than cogently responding. We can't just assume that once we get our moods under control that we're going to be just fine.

It's not just about dealing with our various personality issues either, although that is a large part of what this book is about. Thus, we will take a close look at some of the things that can go wrong in our lives, say when we worry too much or give into our impulses or delude ourselves into thinking we are thinking. We will also look at a few of the destructive outcomes that tend to follow, from social misunderstandings to leading lives of quiet desperation.

Likewise, we will look at our positive attributes, such as creativity and empathy, and all the good things that can happen, from bonding with others to spiritual realizations to peace of mind.

But even then, none of this will make sense to us without coming to terms with a certain sense of psychic unease that nearly all of us experience. It's as if we don't belong here. Where did that feeling come from? You might say this book is an attempt to answer that question. It's a journey that will take us far afield, from our evolutionary beginnings to the cradle of civilization to the present. In the process, we will even imagine the day when Homo Sapiens transition into something else—Homo Optimus, Homo Dystopias, you never know.

If this sounds confusing to you, trust me—I will bring it all back to earth. Plus, at all times I will be framing the narrative in terms of your own bottom line, which is also mine, namely: making sense of why we think and feel and act the way we do.

The path to understanding ranges far and wide. Let's get started ...

PART ONE

NO ONE EVER SAID THIS WAS GOING TO BE EASY

"We are what we pretend to be, so we must be careful what we pretend to
be."
—Kurt Vonnegut, *Mother Night*

1

WHEN THINGS DON'T GO ACCORDING TO PLAN

SOME people can point to a square on the calendar and say this is the day they fell apart. I'm not one of them.

Like many of you, I've always had the feeling of being different, as if born on another planet, with major problems adapting to life on this one. Lord knows, I tried. But that's not always a good strategy.

Finding comfort in my own internal world was how I survived my late child and teen years. By the time I entered adulthood, I was pretty good at it. By the time I hit my mandatory mid-life crisis, I was entirely too good at it.

Take introversion ...

Introversion is a personality trait. People like me draw strength from our own rich internal world. We may successfully relate to other people, and even enjoy getting out, but we find it takes effort and lots of time to recover. Often, we feel that stepping out the door simply isn't worth all the trouble. We would rather be home, inside our own thoughts.

One major catch is that this is hardly the path to world conquest. But this is only a minor inconvenience compared to your brain deciding to terminate its working relationship with you. So, if I must point to a square on the calendar, that would be the second day of January, 1999, living in Connecticut, when my brother turned up to take me to the emergency room. I had been unbearably depressed for at least two years. Now the depression turned life-threatening.

13

"Man is by nature a social animal," Aristotle famously proclaimed, probably to an enthusiastic gaggle of admirers. Somehow, I failed to get the memo.

When I finally got to see a psychiatrist, he simply assumed I had clinical depression and sent me out the door with a sample packet of antidepressant medication. When those pills flipped me into mania, the crisis intervention team that saw me two days later came up with the no-brainer diagnosis of bipolar disorder. Suddenly, I recalled yet another square on the calendar, another day I fell apart, from 11 years before, only this time I had fallen in the direction of "up."

From there, it was fairly easy for me to connect the dots. Bipolar disorder—call it innocent bystander disease. You know, you're merrily tap-dancing down the street, minding your own business, singing a tune, whistling through your pipe. Next thing, life intervenes. Things go crazy, as if you're in a cartoon. Suddenly, before you know it, you find yourself at the bottom of a steam-driven trash compactor with no way out, subjected to a mocking sound track featuring a lot of boing-boing noises, about to be crushed to atoms by unseen forces in the dark.

In the circumstances, it's forgivable to search for meaning, some kind of explanation, a grand theory of everything—if nothing else, a name. Say what you want about diagnostic labels, the term "bipolar" now gave me my grand theory. More importantly, it linked me to a large community of people worldwide. And thanks to the internet, then in its formative years, I lost no time in connecting to them. Soon after, I was connecting face-to-face. Suddenly, I felt a sense of belonging. I no longer felt alone. Through these people—these members of my new tribe—I picked up the insight and wisdom, not to mention companionship, that proved crucial to my recovery.

But even the best of grand theories rarely stand on their own. This is especially true when trying to explain a phenomenon as confusing as our own behavior. If only it were just bipolar, but the people I found myself sharing conversations with inevitably had a lot more going on. Just about everyone was dealing with a co-occurring diagnosis—such as anxiety or attention deficit disorder—and a good many bore the open psychic wounds of past abuse and neglect.

Moreover, everyone experienced major issues in managing stress and getting to sleep.

Inevitably, someone would ask a question that would stump everyone in the group, such as why is it that sometimes we don't feel present in our bodies. Then there were the many issues we faced in controlling our anger and reigning in our impulses and overcoming fear. Predictably, these concerns came up in the context of someone whose world had just turned upside down on them. Troubles at work, financial troubles, relationship troubles. But just as predictably, though, they might also arise in relation to the ridiculously petty. What was going on?

And why did it seem that every question came with the implicit query: Why is it that I don't seem to belong here? What is wrong with me? Why do I feel so different from everyone else?

Slowly, I came to realize that there was more to behavior than just learning to control our emotions. To a person, we just plain saw the world a lot differently than the rest of everyone else. At once, this world could be intensely frightening and wonderful, a dual source of terror and inspiration. The same brain programmed to give in to despair was also capable of producing a Choral Symphony. How do you explain that?

But what got me started in earnest along this path was my own seemingly innocuous trait of introversion. This came up in correspondence some four years following my rendezvous with that 1999 square on my calendar. From there, it was easy to link my dangerous inclination to isolate from the world with my tendency to fall into depression. It was as if one caused the other. So all I had to do was take heed of Aristotle's memo and start acting more like a social animal, right? To a large extent, yes.

The catch was that bipolar still represented the E=MC2 of my own personal grand unified theory of everything. I was looking at introversion through the eyes of someone who had bipolar. But what if I turned it around? What if I viewed my bipolar through the eyes of someone with introversion? How would this change my story?

On my website is an account dating from 1999 of my rendezvous with that earlier square on the calendar, when things fell apart. This took place in Melbourne, Australia, 11 years before, sometime in February 1988. It's a fairly ordinary tale of someone living in his own fool's paradise, in a state of blissful unawareness of the mania that was about to rob him of everything he had worked so hard over the last decade to achieve.

Seen through my new bipolar eyes 11 years after the event, suddenly everything—my whole crazy life—made sense. The account that appears on my website relates what happened that February from that conventional viewpoint. The account I am about to relate here will be much different. Same facts, same events, same disaster, but this time seen through the eyes of an introvert.

15

I hate to admit it, but only now, 18 years after I started to write about my illness, is my bipolar beginning to make any sense. Let's take a look ...

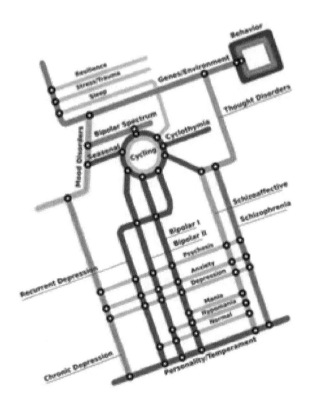

Map of Reality—1: In my first book in this series, NOT JUST UP AND DOWN, I debuted this map of reality from a bipolar perspective. Note how personality and temperament, represented by the bottom line, intersect with various mood states. Also note how through the connecting genes/environment link at the top our moods affect our behavior, and vice-versa.

We will employ a similar map of reality approach in this book, only the map will be drawn from a totally different perspective, with much greater emphasis on the behavior portion, with our moods but a tiny blip on the horizon.

2

WHEN FITTING IN BACKFIRES

LET'S begin ...

It was summer in Melbourne, Australia, and I was living in my own urban Eden. Seven or eight months before, I had moved from New Zealand, full of hope, to start life afresh as a business feature writer on a daily newspaper. My walk into work took me down a tree-lined boulevard, through parks and open spaces, past the Shrine of Remembrance, past the National Gallery and the Performing Arts Centre, past a Zen garden and over a calming expanse of the Yarra River into downtown.

A right turn took me into work. Up the front steps and into a lift and out into a foyer and through double doors into the newsroom. Several months before, while I was sleeping, the markets had gone crazy on Wall Street. When the sun rose in Australia, everyone wanted to sell. Suddenly I was documenting mass hysteria, trying to figure out how people behave. Money only exists in the mind. When we lose faith, it simply disappears. Poof! Gone. Kaput.

Day in, day out, weeks, months, the drama played out. Fortunes were going up in smoke, the financial system was in crisis, no one knew how it would end. Part of my job was to report it. The major part of my job, though, was to make sense of it. The best way to do that was to seek out absurdities. I found a beauty in the form of a Gold Coast property developer, north of Brisbane, who was staging a three-or-four-day outdoor extravaganza that climaxed in an evening concert by Frank Sinatra.

This was one of those fiddle-while-Rome-burns affairs, partly underwritten by a company that I was looking into, a speculative gas giant about to collapse under the weight of its own debt. This was just too good a story to pass up. Of all things, I found myself writing a review of the Sinatra concert, which led the entertainment section the next day. On this job, you had to be ready for everything.

Of the seven or so wheeler-dealers I paid close attention to, by the way, one wound up in jail, another fled the country, two died soon after, another turned into tabloid fodder, another would preside over a string of corporate bankruptcies and a personal one, and another—drumroll—was awarded a knighthood by the New Zealand government.

Meanwhile ...

Back in my urban Eden, I am gaining recognition for my work, and making new friends. The making friends part is rather new to me. In case you were diverted by a text message while reading the previous chapter, I'm an introvert, one who draws strength in my own inner world, away from the madding crowd.

But here I am, in the thick of things, fully committed to succeeding as an Aristotelian social animal, nearly every minute of every day. Failure is always at the top of my mind. Disgrace, banishment. Every day, taking the ride up the lift, in the foyer, just before walking into the newsroom, I stop, steel myself, take a few breaths, anchor my feet into the floor. Then lift one foot and bring it down, do the same with the other. Puff myself up. Breathe once more. Big exhale. Take stock. Wiggle my arms. Walk through the double doors.

Literally, I am willing myself to become an extravert. On the other side of those doors, instead of slinking to my desk and burying myself in breaking news, I pop over to where the other business reporters are congregating. There I am joking, always glad to see them, but also happy to help out and to engage in thoughtful conversation.

It's working, it's working. Become an extravert in 10 easy lessons.

Then to my next challenge of the day. The phone. If you're a guy, cast your mind back to that very first time you asked someone named Deborah Louise Kapinsky out on a date. Something else is kicking in here—social anxiety—which seems to feed on my introversion. In my case, the two seamlessly play off of each other. And here I am, my ability to get stories all depending on cold-calling extremely busy people and convincing them to talk to me. Typically, this involves sweet-talking my way past the Extremely Busy Person's gate-keeper.

I think I can, I think I can ...

Success! Extremely Busy Person has agreed to an exclusive interview. Drop by first thing tomorrow. He's in Sydney, I'm in Melbourne. No problem. So now I have to poke my nose in the office of my editor and pitch my story. If a few minutes earlier, I was an insecure teen talking to a girl on the phone, now I'm that same teen in the principal's office. But this time, I have a certain natural exuberance working for me. We discussed this in great detail in my first book in this series, NOT JUST UP AND DOWN. Technically, exuberance is a personality "trait" that is distinct from a manic or hypomanic (mania lite) "state." But there is a clear overlap, where one may clearly influence the other. And here, talking to my editor, we have another twist: My excitement over having landed the interview has brought my exuberance to the fore, and this is acting as an override against my introversion and social anxiety.

In this state of mind, of all things, it's easy to mistake me for an extravert. So here I am, bursting with excitement, able to frame my pitch to my editor so it sounds like I have the inside scoop on Custer's Last Stand. No way he can say no. Next thing, I'm headed out the door, reservations booked, taxi chit in hand, waving sayonara to my fellow journalists.

See how complicated this gets? See why it can be so difficult figuring out our behavior?

That evening, I'm in full social animal mode with a valued contact and his girlfriend. Good food, good wine. Lots of funny stories, together with story leads. It's as if we've been best friends forever. Next morning, I'm in an office suite overlooking Sydney Harbor, notepad open, recorder on. It all comes naturally to me, of course, intruding into the space of a complete stranger and asking invasive questions.

Later, I call my editor to assure him that his faith in me has paid off. Since this is to be a feature piece, extra preparation will be involved, which means playing well with others back in the newsroom. Meanwhile, back to work.

Life is good. Having successfully broken out of my shell, I no longer have to work so hard at pretending to be an extravert. I'm fitting in. I'm feeling a sense of belonging. I have—finally, after all these years—come home. Then comes the day of that fateful square on the calendar. I walk up the steps, take a ride up the lift, go through my foyer ritual, walk into the newsroom, and hand in my resignation.

With that one move, I have evicted myself from my own Eden.

Holy crap! What on earth went wrong?

What went wrong, of course, was I cycled into mania. My emergent mania, at first my ally in my transformation from introvert to extravert, now seriously impaired my ability to reason. This kicked off a round of strange behavior that quickly escalated from socially awkward to exuberant and eccentric to strange and bizarre to rather frightening. There is no clear line separating weird from crazy, but once I tripped over it, I found myself caught up in forces beyond my control. From there, it was inevitable my life would change.

Fortunately—I use the term loosely—thanks to my unexpected resignation and premature retirement, all my truly mad scenes played out in the privacy of my home, largely out of harm's way. Heaven help had I kept showing up to work.

1986, a year and a bit before my breakdown.

You may be asking yourself how something as seemingly innocuous as a personality trait can actually trigger a mood or anxiety state. I touched on this in the first book in this series, but kept it confined to depressive traits raising the risk of depressive states and manic traits setting the scene for manic states. I also touched upon healthy anxiety begetting panic.

In the context of this book, "trait" is regarded as heritable and tends to remain fairly constant over one's lifetime. Our mood "states," by contrast, are ephemeral, representing a separate and almost alien force. Yet, the two are related. State, in effect, arises out of trait. The two exist in a sort of push-pull relationship.

Often, it is virtually impossible to distinguish one from the other. For instance, "thinking deep" and mild depression may look the same, as does exuberance and hypomania. In my first book, I explored these issues at considerable length. You won't find the answers in any symptom checklist. Rather, we need to be cultivating an awareness of our "true normal."

In that first book, I argued that "normal" is the most overlooked part of our illness. If we think of bipolar as a cycling illness, with our brains in perpetual motion, "normal" is as much a part of our cycling as depression and mania. In this regard, it is a mistake to regard "normal" as the absence of illness. The wheels are always spinning.

We also need to be wary of accepting "normal" as synonymous with some kind of conformity to the norm, as if this were some kind of virtue to which we should all aspire. Rather, it is far more helpful to come to terms with who we really are. On one hand, normal can be an extremely frightening place. On the other, as I explained in my previous book, it is also the repository of all that is good inside us, together with all our hopes and dreams.

In some instances, we need to accept who we are and adapt accordingly. In others, we can give thanks for those parts of us that are true gifts. But first, we need to figure out who we truly are, and that requires rigorous and unflinching self-inquiry.

In my first book, I gave considerable weight to Socrates' injunction to "know thyself." In this book, the emphasis is on Aristotle's observation about man being a social animal. In essence—in reaching some kind of accord with our inner and outer worlds—we need to know those around us with the same degree of intimacy as knowing ourselves.

If only it were just about us. If only it were just bipolar. This concludes Part One. On to Part Two ...

PART TWO

THE GENES-ENVIRONMENT TWO-STEP

"I was a victim of a series of accidents, as are we all."
—Kurt Vonnegut, *The Sirens of Titan*

3

BEYOND "KNOWING THYSELF"

VERY recently, a good friend of mine posted on Facebook a story from the London *Telegraph* (March 28, 2016), bearing this headline: "Mental illness mostly caused by life events not genetics, argue psychologists."

According to the opening paragraphs:

Mental illness is largely caused by social crises such as unemployment or childhood abuse and too much money is spent researching genetic and biological factors, psychologists have warned.

Over the past decade funding bodies like the Medical Research Council have spent hundreds of millions on determining the biology of mental illness. But while there has been some success in uncovering genes which make people more susceptible to various disorders, specialists say that the true causes of depression and anxiety are from life events and environment, and research should be directed towards understanding the everyday triggers.

There we go. Had I only changed my environment—decided to become an accountant or take up the accordion instead of becoming a journalist—I never would have flipped into mania in Australia.

Actually, this is probably true, but that is hardly the whole story. The impression we get from this article is that genes and the environment are two separate entities, as if completely divorced from one another, as if our

25

behavior and mental illness stem from two entirely unrelated sources—genes OR environment.

Moreover, it raises the same old tired nature vs nurture debate, replete with the mistaken notion that one perspective has to be completely true while the other has to be completely false. But scientists speak a very different language. As Robert Sapolsky of Stanford University, who has researched extensively on the impact of stress on animal and human behavior, put it in a 1997 article in *Discover* magazine:

The biological factors that genes code for in the nervous system typically don't determine behavior. Instead they affect how you respond to often very subtle influences in the environment. There are genetic vulnerabilities, tendencies, predispositions—but rarely genetic inevitabilities.

Or, as I would hear it explained to me on numerous occasions, our genes are about how we respond to whatever life happens to throw our way. A personal financial crisis, for instance—something happening in my environment—is not going to automatically make me depressed. Neither is the biology of some rogue gene variation.

But put the two together and turn up the heat, and watch what happens.

Thus, rather than "either-or," we're talking about "both-and," each engaged in an intricate two-step. IF, for instance, I have been dealt a genetic hand that renders my brain less capable of handling stressful situations than most other people in my life, AND a stressful situation happens to materialize, THEN, PERHAPS, I become a sitting duck for depression or anxiety or all manner of maladaptive behaviors, from having an emotional meltdown to not having the will do deal with what has to be dealt with in the here and now to self-medicating with alcohol or drugs.

Without a basic appreciation of this intricate genes-environment two-step—each dance partner influencing the other, the two together influencing but not determining the final outcome—we will never get a grasp of how we think and feel and behave. We need to be nerds and geeks about this sort of thing, and there is no better starting point than a landmark study published in *Science* in 2003. The study had its roots in a "birth cohort" of more than 1,000 infants born in Dunedin, New Zealand in 1972-73.

Had my daughter (who was born in Dunedin) arrived five years earlier, she might have been part of that cohort. Then again, had she been born five years earlier, I wouldn't have been the father.

26

Three decades into the study, researchers led by Avshalom Caspi of King's College surveyed this now adult cohort for recent stressful events in their lives, such as death in the family, losing a job, or breakup with a partner. Then they checked the results against two versions of a particular gene—SLC6A—that regulates the production of the neurotransmitter serotonin.

Bear with me here. I'm about to go seriously nerd-geek ...

The differences in the two versions related to the "promoter" region of this particular gene, stretches of DNA that essentially flip the "on" switch. The short version—"allele"—of the promoter has 14 repeat sequences, the long allele 16. If you're a short allele person, this translates to your neurons producing a little less serotonin than your long allele counterparts. This may be perfectly fine if you lead a relatively stress-free life, but introduce unwanted drama into your world and the lack of those two extra repeat sequences may frustrate your best efforts to manage a challenging situation.

As it turned out, those with the short allele were more than twice as likely to experience stress-induced depression than those with the long allele. Compared to the insignificant statistical blips that turn up in searches for the ever-elusive depression gene or bipolar gene, we are talking big bang here. Not just in terms of an eye-popping result, but in how we view human behavior.

As I heard Daniel Weinberger of the NIMH, who took part in a related study, describe it at the American Psychiatric Association annual meeting that same year, this particular gene "impacts on how threatening the environment feels."

The study Dr Weinberger took part in, by the way, involved scanning the brains of test subjects as they were exposed to fear-inducing images. In the case of those with the short allele, their amygdala—which features in arousal and fear—lit up like a Christmas tree.

Genes working through environment, the environment working through genes. It's always a two-step. It's never "either-or."

Writing in the *American Journal of Psychiatry* at around the same time, Dr Sapolsky explained that the genetics of many psychiatric disorders are based on "if-then" logic. For instance, given certain gene variations, "IF you are exposed to a stressful life event, THEN your risk of depression increases," to the more complex, "IF you are exposed to a stressful life event AND you have a low sense of self-efficacy, THEN your risk of depression increases." (Caps added by the author.)

27

We can easily fill in our own blanks here and add an extra layer or two of complexity to get a more complete story. In my case, having regard to my manic episode described in the previous chapter, given certain gene variations: "IF you are exposed to a stressful life event AND you feel a certain level of discomfort around people, AND you drive yourself too hard, THEN your risk of flipping out increases."

We can even get a bit creative, as in ...

Given the fact that I have a brain that should have been returned to the customer service counter of life five minutes after I was born: IF I decide to take up journalism instead of the accordion AND had I not bonded with a nun in the maternity ward instead of my mother AND if I decide to push my luck being outgoing among people as a street journalist rather than contemplating the pronunciation of "eschatological" in a Trappist monastery THEN my life will crash and burn with the inevitability of a plane taking off on a too-short runway in a low-altitude wind shear.

There is no Owner's Manual for this sort of thing. Typically, we learn from bitter experience. To give the *Telegraph* account its due, this is what their article was driving at—that we need more research to understand these everyday triggers.

In the meantime, we need to be our own experts. If we are seeking to make decent headway in our recovery—this bears repeating over and over —we cannot be too nerdy or geeky about the intricacies of the scientific points of the gene-environment two-step.

Accordingly, Part Two of this book is unapologetically devoted to way more than you ever wanted to know about genes and environment, and everything remotely connected to it. California sea snails? Baboons? British civil servants? You're going to hate me.

In due course, I am hoping to turn you around to my way of thinking. You see, Part Two in large part reflects into how I gradually came into my understanding. We're working on two levels, here, in two different directions. The first starts on the micro level of genes and works its way out to environment. Here, we are working off of the NIMH genes-cells-circuits model. Or, in greater detail: Genes-proteins-cells-circuits-systems-behavior. This is nuts-and-bolts, under-the-hood brain mechanics, but always the environment looms large.

The other—macro—level starts with environment and works its way back to genes. Here, we are talking about evolutionary biology and its off-shoot of evolutionary psychology. One of the missions of the field is to attempt to explain why, in apparent contradiction to the laws of natural selection, we continue to exhibit such an impressive array of maladaptive behaviors— ones that by rights should have been bred out of us millennia before.

It could be that a lot of it has to do with some of our genes operating 200,000 years out of time. For instance, try breathing through your nose during a stressful meeting with your boss when—let's be honest now—you would much rather be embedding a museum-quality flint spear point into the bastard's skull. Indeed, according to evolutionary psychology, this is perfectly normal—that's the way all of us are wired.

Likewise, you can almost say that if we're not getting depressed and anxious or drinking or smoking or imbibing ourselves silly or seeking out shallow pleasures then we're not normal.

This isn't your usual book on behavior. There are plenty of excellent ones out there, many of them by experts who write like journalists or journalists with the insight of experts. These books tend to focus on issues we deeply care about in our daily lives, with valuable information likely to help us in making better choices in our personal relationships and investments and so on.

This book, by contrast, is more concerned with the dynamics of our irrational thinking and behavior than with specific behaviors, per se. Yes, later on, we will be discussing a number of our behaviors in depth, but your level of appreciation will be a lot deeper and wider once you come to the realization that much of it occurs in the context of the many things that can go wrong when the front and back ends of our brains fail to communicate with each other, especially when we're contending with an environment that obdurately refuses to cooperate with us, or a god who refuses to listen, take your pick.

Once you grasp all that—have the nerd-geek stuff down part—you, in essence become your own book. You get to write your own contents, including your own ending.

It's not just about us. When discussing our irrational brains, we're talking about the chronically "normal," as well. They're nearly as nuts as we are. Only—thanks to their majority status—they have a zillion ways of rationalizing their behavior when things go wrong. These are people who, unlike us, are allowed to have three failed marriages with barely a risk of incurring a raised eyebrow. Likewise, they get to walk away from a collapsed project with their reputations fairly intact. Likewise for flipping out and being total jerks.

But when fates happens to deal us a harsh blow—us, not them—we can only scratch our heads in disbelief as we're told that we're being impulsive or grandiose or worse.

Needless to say, we can make a case that the chronically normal are nothing like us. This gets right to the heart of our sense of disconnect. Too often, just when we feel that we are fitting in and getting along, we find ourselves blindsided by behavior that is incompressible to us. Really? Some of you actually enjoy listening to Kenny G?

Who are these people? If we had a chance, would we marginalize them to the fringes of society? Look down on them? Let them know how entirely useless they are? That they only get in our way? That they are holding back the march of civilization?

Alas! Because we're in the minority, we're the ones who have to bend over backward to accommodate them, they, the "linear majority." Our very survival depends on having to please them, to reign in what comes natural to us. Often we succeed brilliantly. We put on a great show. But here's the catch: To do that, we not only need a fully operational brain but fairly benign social surroundings. A hostile environment combined with vulnerable genes gets to us every time.

In order to give you a sense of all that, here in Part Two we will take you on a journey. We start where it all began, four billion years back, when molecules first organized into genes. Inside our DNA is the rulebook of life. Our understanding of human behavior begins here. We ignore the basics at our own risk.

Then we fast-forward to 500 million years ago to cells and circuits, when the most advanced nervous system of the day comprised just 20,000 neurons organized into rudimentary strings called ganglia. If you thought thinking rationally was hard, wait till you find out we do it with essentially the same neurons as sea snails.

Fast-forward another few hundred million years to the higher mammals such as rodents, whose brains possess sufficient complexity to support highly developed systems. Here, we investigate the dialogue between two regions of the brain—the amygdala, which kickstarts our fight or flight response, and the prefrontal cortex which features in our higher thinking.

This tension between brain regions best illustrates the source of all those IF-THEN clauses in our own genome, the ones having to do with how we react to stress in our environment. When it comes to certain basic levels of behavior, it is both mind-boggling and humbling to discover how much we have in common with rats and mice—not to mention skunks.

From here, it is but a hop-step-and-a-jump to the emergence of our early human ancestors, together with the environment they shared with primates, including the baboon. Here, our more advanced intelligence creates new challenges in coping with stress. Instead of just predators and natural disasters, we now have to worry about each other.

By the end of Part Two, we should be able to run every *Jeopardy* category on evolution up to three million years BCE, together with the brain science that goes with it. In Part Three, we apply that knowledge to the here and now. Here, we focus on the issues that hold us back, such as problems dealing with people and workplace stress. Often, we cope in the worst ways possible, such as turning to drugs and alcohol or taking stupid risks.

It's a jungle out there. Not only do we have life in general to contend with, together with our illness, but all too frequently we find our brains reeling from the effects of stress and trauma or the burdens of a related condition such as ADD or OCD. On top of that, we have a plethora of personality issues to contend with, not to mention our own crisis of identity.

From there, in Part Four, we resume our evolutionary chronology. We pick up the narrative at the dawn of man some 200 thousand years ago. We are now the proud owners of a massive brain, plus a possible new killer app. We're on our way up the food chain—that is, once we are able to figure out the operating system.

Our next destination is 12,000 years ago, when we unaccountably developed smaller brains. This coincided with a change from a hunter-gather existence to an agricultural one. In the new world order, perhaps thinking is over-rated.

Fast forward to 6,000 years ago to the beginning of our first cities and civilizations. Bam!—another massive change in our environment. A whole new set of challenges. What could possibly go wrong? Something did—trust me.

By the time we get to the fourth century BCE, we have clear evidence of a world run by sociopaths.

That brings us to our final destination and into an uncertain present. Are our brains up to the challenge? Or has our capacity to think and reason been seriously diminished? Suppose I were to tell you that in our entire evolution, there existed but one Homo Sapien, ever? Of course you would think I'm crazy. But think of the even crazier question I had to ask: Are we truly sapient enough to even refer to ourselves as Sapiens?

This leads into Part Five and what makes us special, including our intuition and creativity and unique sensibilities and our enhanced capacity for empathy. Perhaps we should be thankful we're not part of the linear majority, after all. Perhaps in all that which makes us different, in our profound sense of personal disconnect, lies our salvation.

"Who the hell are we?" we may ask. What on earth are we doing here? Our search for identity begins in earnest.

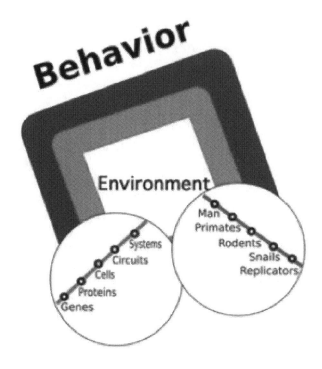

Map of Reality—2: Two complementary views of behavior. To the left, we zero in on the NIMH model from genes to systems and behavior. To the right, we step back to get a long view of evolution. Both perspectives seek to explain behavior in terms of how we respond to our environment

4

FOUR BILLION YEARS AGO: GENES AND PROTEINS

TIMELINE: Second or third day of creation, some time after God separated water from water, but well before teeming creatures appeared in the sea. This was the Golden Age of primordial soup, when molecules first appeared with sufficient complexity to build duplicate versions of themselves from more simple molecular components on hand.

In his 1976 classic, *The Selfish Gene*, Oxford University geneticist Richard Dawkins refers to these biological units as "replicators." His book, which is on just about everyone's most influential books list, popularizes and builds on the work of WD Hamilton and George C Williams, who identified genes as the key units of natural selection.

Many of you better know of Dr Dawkins as that militant atheist who authored *The God Delusion*. If your faith is important in your life, I ask you to bear with me. I am very sympathetic to where you are coming from. Indeed, the four featured personal stories in the first book in this series all involved women with deep faith connections. My next book in this series, on recovery, will validate your faith as a key part of one's overall health and wellness. In the meantime, in this one, I simply ask you to acknowledge that science and religion need not be at odds. In our own minds, we can achieve our own personal reconciliation.

Okay ...

Dr Dawkins asks us to think of the gene as an advanced version of a replicator, one that has developed a protective "vehicle," a survival machine to do its bidding. That survival machine may be as simple as a single-celled organism or as complex as a worm or a human being. Here, we are looking at evolution from the viewpoint of the gene, not the organism—the replicator, never the vehicle.

You may see yourself as the sum total of the 20,000 genes that comprise your genome. The gene, though, sees you as a sort of space ship, built to fend off a hostile environment and stay in one piece long enough to see its passenger(s) through to its manifest destiny of replication and reproduction.

Replication, though, doesn't always go according to plan. A copying error may produce a slightly different version of the same gene. A faithful replication of the copying error means we now have two versions—alleles—of the same gene in circulation amongst the general population, each, technically, in competition.

Thankfully, a species can get along just fine with any number of versions of the same gene in circulation, with virtually no noticeable effect. Or natural selection will weed out any rogues, and with all due speed return matters to the status quo ante. Thus, over the eons, our genetic content has remained remarkably constant.

Every once in a blue moon, though, something completely out of the ordinary takes place. A copying error confers an immediate advantage, and the result can be a game-changer. Something like this happened soon after the domestication of animals in the middle east around 10,000 years ago. There, in the blink of an eye, a lactose-intolerant human population became a lactose-tolerant one. Suddenly, a relative handful of individuals had a new food source which better equipped them for survival and reproduction.

One theory is these dairy farmers migrated into northern Europe with their herds and displaced an earlier generation of hunter-gatherers. There, milk's high concentration of vitamin D conferred an added advantage, where winter sun is in short supply.

Thus, we see a spectacular and exceedingly rare example of a gene variant assuming dominance in a select population and that population taking over a continent. Much later, the history of these people would come to be written in terms of the inevitably of a mighty race—think of Thor with a milk mustache—traveling to distant lands and selflessly taking up the white man's bounty, er burden.

But from a gene's-eye view, we are simply talking about an overachieving random copying error, no more.

Okay, let's stick with this particular random copying error and use it as an example to explore a bit about DNA mechanics. We're going nerd-geek, here. But I'm compassionately sparing you of RNA and a whole boatload of stuff, so please grant me a bit of indulgence ....

Along a double strand of DNA inside the nucleus of the cell, we are able to identify a gene locus. In the case of the ability to digest milk, this would be LCT, whose "promoter region" initiates a chain of events that results in the formation of proteins from amino acids.

In this case, the protein takes the form of the enzyme lactase, which breaks down the lactose sugar found in milk. In the process, the lactase disintegrates back into amino acids, thus setting the scene for a new round of production.

In theory, this process can go on forever, but genes are "regulated"—that is, switched on or off— by neighboring stretches of DNA. In most human populations, lactase production is switched off for good during childhood. But, thanks to a chance variation in how this particular gene is regulated, in certain populations the show goes on. Northern European humans are consuming milk and cheese.

Moving the topic back to human behavior, it's essential that we understand that the same gene-protein mechanics that regulate digestion—or, for that matter, the activity of ancient hydrogen-breathing microbes clustered around hydrothermal vents deep in the ocean—also loom large in our behavior, but with this important proviso, namely: No gene or its variation will "cause" us to become, say, depressed. Rather, as we learned in the previous chapter, genes merely influence our chances of becoming depressed.

To best explain this, consider the neurotransmitter dopamine, which has been implicated in depression and mania, not to mention schizophrenia, ADHD, addictions, and so on, plus assorted behaviors such as novelty-seeking and experiencing pleasure. Our genome contains no shortage of DNA that regulate the many stages of dopamine's life-cycle, from synthesis to neural messenger to metabolic breakdown.

This implies an infinity of things that can go wrong in our cellular mechanics. For instance, the neuron may fail to process the message the dopamine is supposed to be delivering. On a circuits and systems level, one dopamine-saturated region of the brain may be shouting while another, thirsting for the neurotransmitter, is struggling to make itself heard.

Depending on circumstance and location, dopamine can be the hero or the goat. Too much, not enough. It may help make you smarter. Or it may set you up for an emotional crisis. There is actually a gene that appears to have a small influence on both. The gene is known as catechol-O-methyltransferase (COMT). Mechanically, COMT breaks down dopamine and other neurotransmitters. Those with a certain variation metabolize dopamine more slowly, which appears to enhance intelligence. The catch is the same variation may also result in greater emotional instability.

A "good" gene variation or a "bad" gene variation, then? Answer, neither. The gene, itself, is not "consciously" coding for intelligence or emotional instability. It is simply turning out proteins. Maybe the owners of this particular gene variation thrive in their environment. Maybe their chances of attracting a mate are enhanced.

Or maybe not. Or maybe it doesn't make all that much difference.

Recall that short version of the serotonin transporter gene that we discussed in the previous chapter. How, you may ask, could a variation capable of inflicting such spectacular harm have possibly remained in our gene pool?

The answer, should we ever find it, may involve what evolutionary biologists refer to as "tradeoffs." Those genetically prone to sickle cell anemia, for instance, are more likely to be resistant to malaria. Could there some kind of equivalent quid-pro-quo going on here? Researchers have investigated the possibility of our short variation being protective against Alzheimer's, but they are a long way from hitting paydirt. For the present, we are dealing with a confounding mystery.

In the meantime, we need to face the reality that there are only accidents, accidents that in turn survive by more accidents, a series of accidents. Accidents of gene variations, accidents of environment. To illustrate this, let's bring back into the conversation attention deficit disorder, which is all too common in the bipolar population. The condition, which involves a breakdown in dopamine signaling, has a way of turning brilliant minds into underachievers and underperformers.

But cast your mind to centuries ago, in the days before schools and white collar work. Would the gene variations responsible have had the same crippling effect they do today?

This is one of those Zen tree-falling-in-the-forest conundrums: Does a psychiatric disorder—one biologically based—exist if the social environment of the day fails to unmask it?

Perhaps this better explains the mystery of that short allele that sets a lot of us up with stress-induced depression. The genetic vulnerability may exist, but if we are either lucky enough to lead a stress-free life or are particularly skilled in managing our stress, there won't be all that many occasions where we will be putting that vulnerability to the test.

With ADD (or ADHD), because we tend to be talking about our kids, the issue gets particularly heated. This is not the place to get into all the arguments. But I will raise one small point. The other day, I was having a conversation with the mother of a nine-year-old daughter. She casually mentioned she had to have her at school for a 7:30 AM start.

What are we doing to our kids? I could only wonder. Of course their biology is going to protest. Introduce on top of that an otherwise insignificant genetic vulnerability and we're playing with fire.

Everyone has their breaking point. I've already told you how I reached mine. It's not like I was playing with fire—I was simply trying to fit in. It's not like I was in a hostile environment—the people I worked with were very friendly and accommodating. Moreover, my job was extremely rewarding. Everything about my life was good.

But I was an introvert doing an extravert's job. Trying to adapt created its own set of stresses. Something had to give. Something did. Some unknown gene with a particular variation, perhaps. Maybe ten different genes. Maybe a hundred. Who knows? Bam! Accident meets accident. Suddenly, I could no longer rely on my brain to keep me sane.

Next thing, I was driving to my own Armageddon. I managed to pull back just in time, only to retreat into monkish isolation, shut off in my apartment, oblivious to the urbanized Eden just outside my door. If my future looked bleak to me at that point, imagine how my genes must have felt. Here I was, removed from the dating pool. Here they were, removed from the reproductive pool. If my mission on this earth—I had just one job!— was to serve them, then I had let them down completely. In my eyes, I was the most miserable being on earth. From their perspective, I was simply a failed vehicle with 20,000 disappointed replicators.

So it goes ...

5

FIVE HUNDRED MILLION YEARS AGO: CELLS AND CIRCUITS

TIMELINE: Somewhere into the fourth day of creation, with creatures teeming in the sea. Environmental change has resulted in the Cambrian Explosion, which has produced life of new complexity and diversity, including those containing cells specialized into neurons, in turn organized into nervous systems. One order of these marine animals includes sea snails.

Believe it or not, one species of the sea snail would prove instrumental in furthering our understanding of the human brain. The modern side of this story begins just prior to the outbreak of World War II with the arrival of a young refugee to the US, Eric Kandel, from Nazi-occupied Austria.

A survivor of Kristallnacht, many years later he would ask an international audience: "How could a highly educated and cultured society, a society that at one historical moment nourished the music of Haydn, Mozart, and Beethoven, in the next historical moment sink into barbarism?"

Growing up in Brooklyn, young Eric couldn't help but wonder why his childhood traumas became so deeply burned into his memory. To answer his own questions, he qualified as a psychoanalyst, which, he said, at the time was the only discipline devoted to understanding the mind, including its irrational nature. Along the way, though, he stumbled into neurobiology.

As a postdoctoral fellow at the NIMH during the early sixties, Dr Kandel conducted research into the electrophysiology of hippocampal neurons. The hippocampus, which is standard issue in mammalian brains, is involved in laying down memory, which is then offloaded to the cortex for storage. The region is divided into two main sections, which in turn comprises numerous layers of specialized neurons extending their axonal projections into other layers.

The discovery that the hippocampus had to do with memory was purely accidental. In 1953, a neurosurgeon removed a young man's hippocampus to prevent recurring seizures. The operation was a success in the sense that the seizures almost entirely disappeared. The catch was that the patient, who became famous under the alias of "HM," lost nearly all of ten years worth of memories, plus the ability to form new ones.

HM could hold a memory long enough to follow directions to the bathroom. But if he needed to make a repeat visit, he would have to ask again. Basically, HM lost the ability to convert short-term—or working—memory to long-term memory.

Let's investigate further ...

A structure as complex as the hippocampus is not about to readily yield its secrets. Dr Kandel decided he needed a much simpler model to work with. After ruling out crayfish, lobster, flies, and nematodes, among others, he arrived at aplysia californica, the California sea snail.

To Dr Kandel, the creature's small complement of extraordinarily large and distinctively pigmented nerve cells conferred the advantage of easy observation and experimentation. Moreover, nature rarely reinvents the wheel. The neuron found in the snail, including its synaptic structures, is essentially the same neuron we find in humans.

Cue the shock horror. Nothing interesting, Kandel's mentors counseled, could possibly be found in a mere invertebrate, much less have application to higher life forms. But our intrepid researcher was young and brash. Thus, after completing a psychiatric residency at Harvard, off he went to Paris for 16 months to learn about the sea snail. Back in the States, first at NYU in the mid-sixties and then at Columbia University, he devoted himself to the neurobiology of behavior, with the aplysia as his main lab partner.

Compared to the human brain with some 100 billion neurons, the aplysia has but 20,000, about the same number found in your average radio talk show host. These neurons are organized into ten strings of connected cells—ganglia.

Could a system so primitive actually be capable of storing memory? Ah, the joys of nerd-geek inquiry. Memory implies learning, but what on earth would an aplysia see fit to learn? And how would you be able to tell? One giveaway is that snails reflexively withdraw their gills in response to stimuli administered to the animal's spout, an action similar to removing one's hand from a hot object.

Repeated stimuli initiated the synthesis of proteins that converted short-term memory to long-term memory. This, in turn, resulted in greater sensitization to milder stimuli, a form of learned fear. We now actually have a "smart" snail, but also an easily frightened one. Already, in an ancient animal with a primitive nervous system, we are seeing the beginnings of a tension – not to mention seamless integration—between the rational brain and the irrational one.

Stage one of Dr Kandel's research involved mapping the specific neural circuit. This comprised just 24 sensory neurons directly and indirectly connected to six motor neurons. To the surprise of Dr Kandel and his team, in all the snails they examined, they found that the cells and their interconnections always remained the same. What changed, they discovered, were changes in the intensity of neurotransmitter signaling. This was a major finding, which they published in two articles in *Science* in 1970.

But what took place inside the neuron to influence all that signaling in the first place? That was the big question.

In the mid-seventies, Dr Kandel and his team perfected the art of experimenting on cell cultures grown from the larvae of their snails. Now they could observe just three neurons in action—sensory, motor, and interneuron. All the researchers had to do to simulate the tail stimulus effect of the snail was to "puff" micro units of serotonin into the culture. This was as simple a model as one can get.

OK, let's pause and get our bearings. In all likelihood, most of what you have learned about mental illness and behavior has led you to believe that neurons are these cartoon blank circles whose only purpose is to spit out and chew up neurotransmitters such as serotonin and dopamine. The impression is that it is neurotransmitters that do all the real work.

Tell that to the poor neuron. When Kandel and his team kept puffing the serotonin, they found that it activated inside the cell a certain enzyme protein called PKA. Essentially, all hell broke loose. The PKA "translocated" to the nucleus of the neuron, where it recruited another enzyme called MAP kinase ...

40

We'll stop it right there. I think you get the point. It's as complicated as hell in there. As the humorist Bill Bryson explained in his illuminating 2005 book, *A Short History of Nearly Everything*, "never in your life will you have to remind a cell to keep an eye on its adenosine triphosphate levels or to find a place for the extra squirt of folic acid that's just unexpectedly turned up. It will do that for you, and milllions of other things, besides."

Thus, even with three nerve cells—even just two—as long as they are talking to one another, we have sufficient complexity to form a sophisticated neural circuit, one capable of laying down long-term memories. Believe it or not, natural selection has supplied our humble sea-faring friend with the rudiments to the most powerful implement in nature's adaptive tool kit—the ability to learn from experience.

From there, it is easy to visualize our way up the food chain to higher intelligence and the capacity to change our behavior based on thoughtful reflection of our experiences. This may require a much larger and infinitely more complex brain, but on the cellular level everything is played out with essentially the same neurons and circuitry that emerged from the Cambrian Explosion.

But we can also peer up the food chain to see how experience can sabotage our behavior, how our fear can lead to the type of anxiety and trauma that overrides rational thought, to the point where we're living in an invisible shell as real as any snail's. Not only that, it's easy to visualize how our higher intelligence can turn on us and feed into our fears. In an evolutionary blink of an eye, with massive brains, we are about to come up with an infinitude of ways to get distressed. Depression is right around the corner. So is bipolar.

And all the raw ingredients are there, in the nervous system of the sea snail. In his relentless investigation into the learned reflex of a simple sea creature, Dr Kandel helped crack open the secrets of the neuron, and in the process may have answered his own burning questions from childhood. For his efforts, in 2000, he shared the Nobel in Medicine or Physiology.

Five years later, at the 2005 American Psychiatric Association annual meeting in Atlanta, I heard Dr Kandel speak on integrating his first love—psychoanalysis—with his vocation, neurobiology. "A major need of psychiatry in the future," he stated, "is to put the psychotherapeutic arm of psychiatry on the same solid biological footing as the pharmacological aspect of psychiatry."

Molecular genetics and molecular biology, he said, have given us insights that would have been inconceivable 20 or 30 years ago. These advances will revolutionize psychiatry, but hardly eliminate it. Instead, psychiatry will synthesize with molecular biology into what he describes as "the new science of the mind."

What would Freud have to say about all that? Let's ask ...

6

SIXTY-FIVE MILLION YEARS AGO: SYSTEMS, STRESS, AND BASIC BEHAVIOR

TIMELINE: Somewhere into the fifth day of creation. Thanks to the fortuitous arrival of a comet and its resultant firestorm some 65 million years ago, small mammals now wander freely on the land, with no fear of dinosaurs. Today, rodents—which include rats and mice—comprise forty percent of all mammals. They are virtual Darwinian survival machines, capable of adapting to the most extreme and bizarre of environments. Thus, you will never find them on any endangered species list. Indeed— when the dust has cleared--they will be the ones writing our eulogies.

When it comes to studying humans, rats and mice serve as admirable stunt doubles. As well as possessing miniature versions of our organs, they also come equipped with a similar "triune brain" to ours—a marvel of evolutionary retrofitting--with two layers of mammalian grey matter jury-rigged to a reptilian brain stem.

Cortex-wise, these little guys may lack the neural horse-power to work out differential equations. But there's enough there under the skull to enable them to make the course corrections they need to make to adapt on the fly. Just mess with their cheese supply and watch what happens.

Emotion-wise, you may not be able to exactly ask a rat how it's feeling, but treat the poor creature miserably—remove it from its mom, shock it, prod it, toss it in water, suspend it by its tail, place it in a crowded cage, drop it in an open space, run it through mazes, play it Kenny G music—and simply observe what happens.

Now do the same thing to a human kid: Expose him to abuse and deprivation, ship him off to fight in a foreign war, place him in a toxic work environment, throw in the relationship from hell, rain down financial worries, make him jump through hoops, play him Kenny G music—and see what happens.

Expose any mammal—four-legged or two-legged—to that kind of abuse and see what happens. This takes us straight into Eric Kandel's new science of the mind, for it is here, where worry meets brain cell, that Freud and neuroscience truly converge.

Of all things, Freud's career bears an uncanny parallel to that of Dr Kandel's, only in reverse order. The man we regard as the father of psychiatry and the founder of psychoanalysis actually started out as a neuroscientist examining the nervous systems of crayfish and other sea creatures. His lab work during the 1880s led to the principle of the neuron as the foundation of the nervous system. Had he pursued this line of work, he might have established an entirely different reputation as one of the fathers of neuroscience. Instead, he started seeing patients.

In 1895, he set out his intentions of mapping human behavior to the nervous system, but considered his first attempt a failure, and abandoned the project completely. Instead, in 1900, he published *The Interpretation of Dreams*, with no reference whatsoever to the physical brain. The rest is history.

By the end of the Second World War, virtually every university psychiatric department in the US was in thrall to Freud. Thus, when the American Psychiatric Association set to work putting together its first diagnostic bible—the DSM-I of 1952—it was no surprise that commonly acknowledged mental illnesses such as manic-depression and schizophrenia were expressed in terms the Wizard of Id would have approved. Thus: "manic depressive reaction" and "schizophrenic reaction."

The descriptive sections to these diagnoses were filled with Freudian notions of neurosis and psychosis, with ample reference to defense mechanisms and maladaptations. From a modern perspective, the idea that a biologically based illness such as bipolar could possibly be the result of some kind of maladaptive reaction—say as the result of bad parenting—was nothing short of ludicrous. As if, simply through a revelatory insight, we could just will away our depressions and manias.

But a more sympathetic reading reveals something far more sophisticated going on. According to the DSM-I, our so-called reactions "are as much determined by inherent personality patterns, the social setting, and the stresses of interpersonal relations as by the precipitating organic impairment."

It's what we've been discussing all along, namely what happens when our genes and biology meet our environment. What we're missing is a coherent integration. It was as if psychiatry back then viewed the mind as an entity distinct from the brain, and the brain as some mysterious black box.

While Freud was exploring how the unconscious mind influenced human behavior, a new generation of biologists began poking into that black box. In 1915, the Harvard physiologist Walter Cannon came up with the concept of "fight or flight." Building on that, the Austrian-Canadian endocrinologist Hans Selye hit upon an accidental discovery. As a dutiful but clumsy young medical student in the 1920s, Selye kept dropping the rats he handled and was forced to chase them around the lab with a broom.

Little did he know that he was conducting his own pioneering experiments. As it turned out, the badly stressed rats that wound up on his dissection table had unusually large adrenal glands and small lymphatic structures, plus peptic ulcers. At first Selye thought he had discovered a new hormone, but when he compared his poor rats to a batch he hadn't had a chance to drop, he knew he was onto something new. Such is the nature of scientific discovery.

Over the decades, with the rat as his principal lab partner, Selye would map the hypothalamic-pituitary-adrenal axis system (HPA axis)—the neuroendocrine pathway responsible for pumping adrenaline and glucocorticoids into the bloodstream and thus activating the body's fight or flight response.

In 1936, he identified "general adaptation syndrome," which broke down the stress response into three stages: Alarm (involving fight or flight), resistance (involving attempts to adapt to continued stress), and exhaustion (where illness sets in).

The term stress, by the way, did not enter into medical discourse until 1950, when Selye made note of it in a scientific paper. Selye, incidentally, was nominated ten times for the Nobel in Medicine, but came up empty on each occasion.

Moving on ...

In the 1960s, Paul MacLean of the NIMH identified the brain's lower mammalian layer as the "limbic system," involved in the processing of emotions, as opposed to the cortical layer associated with higher functions.

From there, starting in the 1980s, Joseph LeDoux of NYU zeroed in on the limbic system's amygdala and mapped its incoming connections from various sensory and cognitive pathways and out via other pathways into the cortex, basal ganglia, and HPA axis. Working with rats, Dr LeDoux successfully implicated the amygdala in the processing of arousal and fear and anger.

To see how this works, all we need to do is place two mammals in an enclosed space. One strides confidently down the center of the arena, not a care in the world. The other beats a hasty retreat into an adjacent space and manages to close a door. One of the mammals is a skunk, the other human—me, in fact. Guess which mammal is which.

Give yourselves a moment to adjust. Ready? The narrative is about to turn into an action-thriller, with a nerd overlay, a sort of James Bond for intellectuals. Cue soundtrack. Roll footage ...

Title: Two Amygdalae and a Door.

As fellow mammals in confrontation mode, our respective brains were now operating almost identically. Our limbic systems were both alerting us to danger and governing our immediate reactions. In particular, the amygdala was kickstarting both of our fight or flight responses and sending alarms up the line to our respective cortical regions. Already, I was in a heightened state of awareness bordering on panic.

Here I was, on my side of the door, adrenaline flowing, glucocorticoids gushing, neurons zapping, heart pounding, breathing accelerating, digestive sugars pumping raw energy into the muscles. Within the space of one microsecond, I was primed to fight like a kung-fu master on steroids or run faster than Michael Phelps can swim. But millions of years of evolution never anticipated the exigencies of modern living gone bad, namely me trapped in my bedroom with a skunk just outside.

I needed to think things through.

But our brains don't work that way. Survival depends on instant reaction. Only later does actual thinking enter into the picture. Which explains why in the modern world we do stupid things such as panic and fly off the handle and start fights and fall in love and otherwise act against our own best interests.

Moreover, the cortical areas don't automatically take over, even when they do come back online. In theory, the thinking parts of the brain are supposed to modulate the reactive parts of the brain, but too often it works the other way around.

"Bang on the door! Make noise!" That was what my limbic-influenced cortical regions were telling me. Bad thinking.

Pepe Le Pew, in the meantime, was working off the exact same standard-issue amygdala as mine, only the "end" result of an alarmed reaction, from my point of view, would be far more consequential and dramatic.

So here was the trick: Under no conditions could my amygdala set off his amygdala, and the only thing to prevent that from happening was for my cortex to take charge.

Scratch-scratch-scratch. Pepe was now on the hardwood floor just outside my room.

Scratch-scratch. The only thing separating me from a living weapon of mass destruction was the bedroom door—a door with a cat flap.

Bang on the door! Make some noise!

No! Cortex to the rescue. "Just wait!" said the voice of reason with not one second to spare. "He's headed out the other door. One that also has a cat flap. All you have to do is breathe."

A sound. The cat flap, but not in fully committed mode. Slowly, carefully, I opened the bedroom door a crack and peered out. The skunk was stalled three-quarters of the way through the cat door, tail inside, fully upright.

"Hurry him up!" said the panic-influenced part of my brain. "Bang on something! Now!"

"Wait, you idiot!" my voice of reason cut in. "In case you haven't noticed, the operating end of this walking violation to the Geneva Convention has not yet left the building! Don't—I repeat—don't! Don't, don't, don't ..."

One Mississippi, two Mississippi ...

An eternity, another one, and another. Then—the welcome sight of a furling tail disappearing through the door followed by the definitive sound of the final flap. Free at last!

My elation at having prevented a "situation" from escalating into nuclear destruction was dampened by the realization that skunks think I'm a joke. Clearly, this is going to require years of intensive therapy to get over.

The shame! I won't allow them to make a movie out of this. If Spielberg calls, tell him I'm busy.

To bring this back to earth ...

A 2010 International Society of Bipolar Disorder Neuroimaging Task Force led by Stephen Strakowski of the University of Cincinnati concluded that amygdala activation is present across all mood states in bipolar disorder, including mania, hypomania, and depression. In addition, various studies the task force cited showed a deficit in the capacity of the frontal regions of the brains of bipolar subjects to suppress their overactive amygdalae.

To freely interpret, where you find our brains veering out of control, heading into depression or mania, you will find an amygdala that works way better than it was meant to. Not only does this exert a profound impact on our behavior, it tremendously complicates the course of our illness. Be safe, be careful—and, for heaven sakes, watch out for skunks.

7

THREE MILLION YEARS AGO: SYSTEMS, STRESS, AND SOCIAL RELATIONSHIPS

TIMELINE: The dead of night between the fifth day of creation and the sixth. Our distant hominin ancestors—australopithecines—are sharing the same jungle and savannah habitats as our primate cousins. Among this population is "Lucy," whose fossilized remains would one day gain her enduring fame. Anthropologists, however, would deny her the "homo" status that would define her as one of us, a species of human.

It's not hard to see the reason for her exclusion. In appearance, she resembles a chimpanzee who just happens to walk upright, of similar height and with the same size brain. Moreover, she spends a good deal of her time in trees, almost certainly as part of a harem dominated by an alpha male.

But if she is not technically a human, she is not strictly an ape, either. Nor is she descended from one. Rather, she and the chimps and baboons in her vicinity share a common ancestor from another three million years in the past. If you can imagine a family tree, we see two separate branches —ape and man—growing from an older limb representing our distant common ancestor.

This bears emphasis. We do not see a human branch sprouting from the ape branch. Contrary to common misconceptions about evolution, we are not descended from apes, though it may look that way. Genetically, Lucy and her chimp cousins are an almost perfect match, but the two are now headed down entirely separate paths. In a matter of generations, after a few million years of apparent genetic stasis, Lucy's descendants—or that of some other closely related species, perhaps unknown to us—will receive that rare evolutionary upgrade that will change everything.

This is about to happen in the form of a random copying error that produces three extra, but not exact, duplicates of the gene SRGAP2. Together, these copies slow down brain development, but in a way that results in denser neural connections.

The emergence of this gene 2.5 million years ago corresponds with australopethicine's transition to Homo Habilis and the use of crafted stone tools. Humankind is on the road to higher intelligence and world domination. But for the time being Lucy and her family are just trying to get through another day on the savannah, rocks and stone slivers in hand, waiting their turn around an antelope carcass. Once the jackals and hyenas leave, Lucy and kin will scrape off whatever flesh is sticking to the bones and help themselves. They will also smash open the bones and feast on the marrow.

At least some of them will. Let's bring back into the conversation Robert Sapolsky, who we first encountered in Chapter Three.

Dr Sapolsky has studied stress and behavior as both a neuroscientist specializing in the hippocampus and as a primatologist tracking baboons in the wild. In a 2007 interview posted on the Stanford University website, he posits that humans, apes, and monkeys are way too intelligent for their own good. "Primates are super smart and organized just enough to devote their free time to being miserable to each other and stressing each other out," he said.

Fish and birds and reptiles and mammals secrete the same stress hormones we do, but they don't endanger their metabolisms the way people and primates do. Certain animals may be social, but they don't have complex emotional lives. According to Dr Sapolsky: "It's not until you get to primates that you get things that look like depression."

In the 2004 edition to his best-seller, *Why Zebras Don't Get Ulcers*, Dr Sapolsky points out that in dealing with the crisis at hand—such as being chased by a lion—the body in essence ceases work on its long-term building projects (such as making bone marrow, digesting food, or thinking about the future) in favor of more immediate concerns, such as stoking the heart and lungs, stimulating neural circuits, and delivering instant energy to the muscles.

Soon enough, with the resolution of the crisis, all systems reset to normal. Essentially, the body works to maintain a state of equilibrium, a process known as homeostasis. Paradoxically, it accomplishes this by allostasis. For instance, in anticipation of even routine physical activity, glucose levels will temporarily spike way above normal to diabetic readings.

But continued exposure to stressful situations can bring on "allostatic load," where overburdened systems fail to reset to normal. Starvation, for instance, will result in your body storing fat rather than burning it. This is one reason, incidentally, why virtually all diets fail. You may think you're battling against your own lack of will power. But you need to give yourself a break—you are really up against a much more powerful force of nature.

So thanks to ridiculous social demands and failed diets, we now have low self-esteem to gnash our teeth over, which is the very point Dr Sapolsky is making. Thanks to our state-of-the-art primate brains, we have turned ourselves into perpetual worrying machines, dealing with one manufactured emotional crisis after another. Literally, we are thinking ourselves into chronic stress.

You might refer to chronic stress as a sort of global body disease that rampages everywhere, striking at the weakest link. For instance, allostatic load may provoke our immune system into a state of perpetual high alert. One effect, according to Dr Sapolsky, is one of your guys getting shot in a friendly fire accident. The immune system mistakes part of you for something invasive, and "you've got yourself an autoimmune disease."

On and on it goes, systems in crisis—hypertension, heart disease, diabetes, and so on.

In addition, all manner of brain function is impaired. According to Husseini Manji—formerly in charge of researching mood disorders at the NIMH—at the neural level some of those glucocorticoids released into the blood by fight or flight bind to glucocorticoid receptors on neurons in the amygdala, hippocampus, PFC, and other brain regions. This sets off the release of the excitatory neurotransmitter glutamate. Too much glutamate, though, can literally excite neurons to death, or substantially weaken them, making them sitting ducks for the next catastrophe.

It doesn't stop there. Weakened neurons literally drop out of circulation, compromising communication along neural circuits and ultimately entire brain systems.

The hippocampus is of particular interest to researchers. We already know it is involved in laying down memories. It is also implicated in mood and emotions. Intriguingly, it is the one area of the brain where new brain cell growth—neurogenesis—takes place. In the lab, Dr Sapolsky discovered that stress essentially shuts this process down. Brain scans of victims of

PTSD, for instance, reveal smaller hippocampal volumes than those without PTSD.

In 2000, Ron Duman and his team at Yale discovered that in rats antidepressants actually stimulate neurogenesis. Not only that, the "depressions" in these same rats lifted.

Yes, depression may be all in your head. But we're talking about a head that is forced to operate with distressed neurons often unable to talk to one another. Depression, then, is as physical as a blocked artery.

Now imagine other areas of the brain in crisis, ones fingered in bipolar disorder, such as the prefrontal cortex, the anterior cingulate (a key brain hub), and the striatum (tied to the dopamine system). According to Dr Manji, it is helpful to regard our illness as "associated with atrophic changes in discrete brain regions."

Our brain cells in key regions are taking a beating, in other words. A lot of this may have to do with gene variations involved in the maintenance of the cell, such as brain derived neurotrophic factor (BDNF), which regulates a protein that helps mediate neural survival, inhibit cell death, and modulate synaptic neurotransmitter activity.

Imagine, now, stress-induced glucocorticoids initiating various glutamate cascades that excite the neuron to the point where BDNF and other proteins can't do their job. Once we've reached this stage, to freely interpret Goodwin and Jamison in the 2007 edition of *Manic-Depressive Illness*, bipolar essentially takes on a life of its own.

What we now know about the effects of chronic stress on our neurons and neural circuits lends strong support to the "kindling" theory of bipolar. Basically, the dynamics of allostatic load have taken us past the point of no return. Our brains have changed too much to allow a homeostatic return to "normal." Our new normal now involves extreme sensitivity to nature's cycles—whether seasonal or daily—where our energy levels ebb and flow like an unpredictable current and our depressions and manias seem to come out of nowhere.

We can construct similar scenarios for other psychiatric disorders and conditions—of chronic stress changing our brains forever—often to the point where psychiatric labels become virtually meaningless. Consider, for instance, just two of the things that can go wrong in two brain regions we have touched on—an amygdala sensitized to the point of sending false alarms that won't shut off and a prefrontal cortex unable to send a convincing modulating signal back to the amygdala—and we have a human being with messed-up wiring, call it whatever you want, depression, anxiety, ADD, bipolar, borderline personality disorder—at a loss in how to negotiate even the most routine social situations. We're back into Freud's world now, not to mention Darwin's. From their perspective, we're failing to adapt to our environment. It could be the same old environment, or one that has suddenly turned on us.

It doesn't get any more primal than this. Adapt or die. Meanwhile, on the savannah ...

If you're lucky enough to be a baboon, you only have to work three hours a day for your basic needs, and predators are not a major concern. As it turns out, even in paradise, we succeed in finding ways to make ourselves miserable. Baboons, with their extreme sexual dimorphism (the males are much larger than the females) and alpha dominance hierarchies, absolutely specialize in terrorizing each other, and they have plenty of free time to do it. Says Dr Sapolsky: "They're just like us. They're not getting done in by predators and famines, they're getting done in by each other."

Imagine poor Lucy, a few hundred yards distant from her tree-dwelling baboon cousins, out in the open under a hot African sun, about to break open her antelope bone and help herself to the nutritious marrow. Imagine some overfed alpha asshole of her species, ripping the bone out of her hand.

Meanwhile, back at the office ...

Suppose you must endure a job you hate, day after day, year after year. In 1967, researchers began tracking 18,000 male British civil servants over a ten-year period. A second study (begun in 1985 and still ongoing) is tracking 10,000 male and female British civil servants. The two studies are known as the Whitehall Studies.

The clear finding from both studies was that mortality rates turned out to be far higher for those in the lower echelons of the British civil service than the upper echelons, even after controlling for lifestyle and other factors. One would think that those in senior management would experience a lot more stress than those lower down. But think again. Those poor souls at the bottom have little or no control over their situation. They have no choice but to sit there and take it. Upper level employees, by contrast, have far more say in how they go about their day.

It's not that the alphas necessarily get off scot-free. High-stakes competition brings on its own set of stressors. If you're an alpha baboon, for instance, and your fiercest rival decides to take a nap next to you, let's put it this way—you're not going to get much sleep.

But who wants to be a beta? In any species that places a premium on strength and aggression, the jock is king. The lot of the beta baboon is a lifetime of being bullied. The best they can hope for is some ameliorating social grooming. Sadly, these poor creatures lack the option of joining an alternative social structure.

By contrast, humans have the resources to create their own social networks. The lowly office drudge, for instance, may rule the roost in her local judo club. The hapless nerd can always find other nerds to hang out with. By nature, we are social animals, and our ability to use this trait to our advantage is the single greatest contributing factor to our health, physical and mental.

The best support for this comes from the longest-running set of studies on a human population, the Grant Study, tracking young men from Harvard, and the Gleuck study (later incorporated into the Grant study), following disadvantaged young men from inner city Boston. Both studies began in the late 1930s and are still ongoing. One of the young men in the Grant Study was JFK.

George Vaillant, the man who headed up the Grant Study from 1972 to 2005, trained as a Freudian psychoanalyst. At age 10, his father committed suicide. He was the last person to see his father alive. We pick up the narrative from Joshua Wolf Shenk, who wrote a penetrating article in the June 2009 *Atlantic*.

As Mr Shenk describes it, Dr Vaillant's main interpretive lens has been the psychoanalytic metaphor of "adaptations" (also called "defense mechanisms"), a sort of psychic analogue to the type of inflammatory responses that the body employs to protect itself against physical damage, say by triggering the blood to clot around an open wound.

In our interior life, one extreme form of this adaptation, psychosis, can actually make reality bearable, but will not exactly win friends and influence people. Neither will "immature" adaptations, such as acting out or passive-aggression. "Neurotic" defenses such as intellectualization (using thinking to avoid feeling) are fairly normal, but we're better off aiming for "mature." Mature responses would include altruism, humor, and finding healthy outlets for your emotions.

If you're picking up a theme regarding how we respond to stressful situations in dealing with people, you are on the right track.

Dr Vaillant took over the study with these men now into middle age, which is when things started to get interesting. The privileged Harvard men, for instance, who had entered the study mentally and physically healthy, were now showing signs of wear and tear. Many had achieved success, but by age 50, a third had met Dr Vaillant's criteria for mental illness.

Nevertheless, as the men got older they proved more successful in employing mature defenses over immature ones. These mature defenses translated into forging strong social connections, and here it gets especially interesting. For instance, as we get older, our ability to maintain meaningful relationships has a greater role to play in our longevity than cholesterol.

In fact, healthy relationships are the key to a long life. This was the message Dr Vaillant's successor, Robert Waldinger, hammered home in a 2015 TED Talk. According to Dr Waldinger: "The clearest message that we get from this 75-year study is this—good relationships keep us happier and healthier. Period."

Loneliness kills. (Note to self: Keep working on my introversion.) People connected to friends and family and community are happier and healthier and live longer.

"The good life," Dr Waldinger concludes, "is built with good relationships."

Even we deserve to be happy.

This concludes Part Two. I trust by now you are on board with the nerd-geek stuff. In Part Three, we will apply our new understanding to the issues we face in our daily lives.

PART THREE

STUFF THAT IS HOLDING US BACK

"And nearer and nearer the zeppelin came."
—Kurt Vonnegut, *Breakfast of Champions*

8

STUCK IN OUR RECOVERY

"WHAT is holding you back most in your recovery?" I asked readers on my blog *Knowledge is Necessity* in March 2009. What motivated me to pose the question was my observations from eight years of participating in and facilitating depression and bipolar support groups in three states.

There, I would witness individuals who seemed to be on the verge of breaking through to recovery, with the hope of returning to their old lives. or some reasonable approximation of it. But they just couldn't get there. Week after week, they seemed to hit one brick wall after another.

"Stuck in their recovery," was how I used to phrase it. To what degree did they hold their illness accountable? I wondered. Accordingly, I prepared a one-question survey with nine possible answers. Readers were free to check off as many as they wished. (169 respondents accounted for 490 answers, averaging nearly three answers per person.)

My main finding stunned me: Only a third replied that unresolved illness symptoms—all those depressions and manias—accounted for what was holding them back. Another way of phrasing that: A full two-thirds felt they had their moods under control, to the point where their ups and downs no longer significantly interfered with their lives.

On reflection, though, this pretty much validated what I had observed in support groups. There had to be other reasons for their being stuck, and my second major finding confirmed it:

The answer that drew by far the most respondents—exactly half—were "fears/difficulties in dealing with people." Closely related to this (with a third filling in this blank) was a "bad living/work, etc situation."

We're back once more in the world of Darwin and Freud—not to mention Robert Sapolsky—where our challenging social environments play havoc with our genetic vulnerabilities. My readers were telling me, in effect, that people were a harder puzzle to solve than their illness. Since every criteria for success in this world, not to mention our mental well-being, rides on getting the social animal part of the script right, this was hardly a good sign.

It's easy to see how it happens. All it takes is one severe episode—manic or depressive—to remove us from mainstream society. Look what happened to me. I'm guessing you have a similar story. Endure the post-episode social fall-out long enough—the rejections, the humiliations, the put-downs—and see how long your confidence holds up. Next thing, you're isolating. Next thing you're viewing social situations as a threat, or at least not worth the effort.

From there, it's all downhill. One third reported an "inability to manage fears, impulses, etc apparently unrelated to [our] illness." And a third again reported bad personal habits and making excuses.

All these are issues the general population faces as well, but for us the stakes are a lot higher. If we fail to get our act together, do the things we need to do to keep up appearances and get back on track, we're stuck in limbo forever. But try organizing your day when your brain feels overwhelmed by even the smallest task. Try lining up job interviews when you're terrified to walk out the door. Try making a good social impression when you haven't had a real conversation in over a month.

Meanwhile, outside your door, it's as if everyone has been recruited into a social behavior experiment designed to disorient you or provoke a reaction from you. One friend of mine—an Ivy League graduate—got abused by her psychiatrist for wearing Bermuda shorts to her appointment.

Who was the sadist who came up with that experiment?

And who were the evil minds who coached the people around you to tell you that you were manic when you simply laughed or had a good idea, or that it was your bipolar talking and not you when you were justifiably upset?

Yeh, I can picture the review board who approved that experiment, snickering in their leather chairs. Yeh, let's take a real person and not acknowledge her feelings, disapprove of her every breath, deprive her of her sense of feeling human. Let's see how long it takes to break her spirit.

And is there a degree course where people are trained to give you ridiculous advice or insult the hell out of you and then tell you that they just want you to be happy? Or that they don't want to see you back in the hospital?

And how do we account for all the deniers who suddenly turn up in our lives, you know, the ones who say horrible things to us and then deny it, or, under duress, finally acknowledge the content of what they said is more or less true but then claim you interpreted it all wrong.

Hey, you're the one who no longer has a job who is about to be kicked out of your home. What do you know? It's like we're living in an episode from *The Twilight Zone*. This has to be part of an ingenious social experiment, right?

Walk into any support group and you can see the human toll. For one, we might develop a dependency mindset. Call it a form of learned helplessness. In the blink of an eye, we have transitioned from the world of paychecks and investments and the occasional pat on the back to benefits and family charity and the evil eye. It's an existence guaranteed to keep us in poverty and strip us of our sense of self-worth, but it's one that is perversely easy to adapt to.

Once that happens, the world we're looking to get back into comes across as even more frightening, more difficult to access. We become fearful. We adopt avoidant behavior. We start making excuses. Next thing, we're nurturing a sense of victimhood.

Or it could be that we are still putting up a fight, which breeds its own set of difficulties. Maybe instead of banging our stubborn heads against the same spot on the same wall, we need to come to terms with our own limitations. Maybe we have to face the fact that we can never go back to our old lives. Maybe we have to learn to scale down our expectations, even if this means going on disability. Otherwise, we could be setting ourselves up for endless rounds of disappointment, which we can interpret as another form of victimhood.

Either way, helpless or defiant, we still have our miserable days to get through. We may turn to drugs or alcohol. We may neglect our personal hygiene and basic health. One bad habit piles up on top of another. Some of us, desperate to find temporary relief from our psychic pain, take up thrill-seeking or other risky behaviors—unprotected sex, picking fights, and so on.

Our setbacks have taken their toll. In particular, our skills in reading people have been greatly diminished. Put-downs and humiliations have a way of doing that to you. Negotiating even a simple conversation becomes a major effort. We open our mouths when we need to keep them shut, and vice-versa. In our frustration, we may lash out. In our resignation, we may withdraw into our shells.

We're the betas in the pack now, forever trying to ingratiate ourselves to the alphas, ever eager to please. Of course we're going to mess it up. We overcompensate, try too hard. Or we lurk on the fringes, fearful of engagement, but hoping against hope something good will happen.

All this and more are what my readers in my poll are telling me. I've seen it in support groups, I've seen it in my friends. No doubt, you have lived through at least some of it. I certainly have.

It's the whole social stress genes-environment two-step we have been talking about from the very beginning. Examine the stress component more closely and we uncover both anxiety and trauma. Literally everyone with a bipolar diagnosis is walking around with generous portions of both. Try having a normal conversation, trying feeling at ease with yourself and around others, when your fear circuits are constantly messing with your mind.

Stress also has a way of throwing our thinking off-line. We fail horribly on tests involving performing cognitive tasks under pressure. Transpose this situational deficit to social settings. Here you are, trying to navigate your way through a room full of strangers when your brain suddenly stops cooperating with you. To make life even more complicated, you may be laboring under the burden of attentional deficits. Try staying present in the here and now and all that implies—fully engaging with the people around you, keeping track of your social commitments, and so on—when your frontal lobes start drifting out through the top of your head.

Then there is pleasure to contend with. Think of pleasure as the flip side of fear, an emotion that both guides your thinking and throws it off, that motivates you to do your best as well as your worst, a force of nature so powerful that you find yourself consumed by it, a slave to its manifold addictive charms.

Or you may find yourself terrorized by your own thoughts, ones your brain circuits refuse to release. Heaven help should you find yourself compelled to act on them.

Then there is the whole issue of personality. Yes, our gifts can make us the envy of all those hopeless stuck-in-muds who can only appreciate a sunset as a desktop screen-saver. We will be exploring these superpowers in great depth in Part Five—our intuition and creativity and enhanced capacity for empathy and all the rest. But this section is devoted to those parts of us that hold us back, and it's not pretty. Nature, unfortunately, is far too generous in doling out negative personality traits. Some of us may be contending with a co-occurring personality disorder. All of us are dealing with personality issues in abundance.

It's never just bipolar. And it's never just about us, either. Not only do we have to deal with our own issues, we are forced to contend other people's issues, as well. We're back once more inside our *Twilight Zone* social experiment. Earth can be a very strange place. Sometimes, you just can't win. But we have to adapt. Those are the rules. No waivers, no exemptions.

One quick reminder: Although our next chapters are devoted to the issues that keep us stuck in our recovery, we won't be discussing the practical tips and tricks involved in getting us unstuck. That is for my next book, which will have "recovery" in either the title or subtitle. To repeat what I said in the preface: Be patient—that book is on the way. In the meantime, bear in mind: Recovery is a complete nonstarter without understanding.

First, let's acknowledge our suffering, the hells we've been through, the privations and humiliations we've endured. Allow yourself to grieve, to mourn the life you lost. Allow yourself to rage against the world, to rail against the sheer injustice of it all. Allow yourself to despair. It's probably not going to get better any time soon.

Embrace your suffering. It's your key to wisdom and understanding. It's your teacher, your guide, your counselor. Suffering is inevitable. It's part of the human condition. But to suffer without learning is a wasted opportunity. To persist in suffering and not learning is a wasted life.

9

THREE TALES OF SOCIAL ANXIETY

IN PART TWO, we discussed what may happen in the brain and to our behavior when a hostile environment acts on vulnerable genes. One inevitable outcome is anxiety. In 2013, the DSM added this specifier to depression, hypomania, and mania: "With anxious distress." As I described it in the first book in this series:

> *You know the feeling. You're keyed up, on edge, burdened by worry, barely holding it together. Imagine yourself outside your car with a ticking nuclear bomb in the trunk with your keys locked inside—that sort of describes it.*
>
> *The likely connecting link is stress. Think of the amygdala—that tiny part of the brain which kicks off fight or flight—launching a plate of spaghetti against the wall. In this context, some of what sticks is mania/hypomania, some of it anxiety. Once again, keep in mind that our brains are not organized according to DSM categories.*

As I reported in that book, three in every four individuals with bipolar also experience a form of full-blown anxiety. But we need to keep in mind that our brains don't simply ignore less severe forms of this condition. Hence the long-overdue DSM acknowledgement, a full century after the pioneering diagnostician Emil Kraepelin made similar observations. Virtually all of us with bipolar deal with some level of anxiety.

64

That first book took a more global view of the condition. There, I described my panic in taking a road test, after not driving for 30 years. Here, where the focus is on us coping as social animals, it's more appropriate to zero in on social anxiety. You saw some of this on display in Chapter Two, back in Australia in 1988, where I was contending with being an introvert performing an extravert's job. Social anxiety is a different phenomenon, but each clearly feeds off the other. In my case, introversion is a refuge, social anxiety a prison.

This is the happy story of my escape from that prison, told in three episodes. Let's rewind back to the late summer of 2000 ...

* * *

It's been 19 or 20 months since my diagnosis, and I have been putting out a depression and bipolar newsletter for a bit more than a year. One of my subscribers, Zach, emails me with the suggestion that I come up to Boston for the annual Depression and Bipolar Support Alliance (DBSA) conference. Back then, the organization was called the National Depressive and Manic Depressive Association (NDMDA), or what I refer to today as the full mouthful.

I hesitated in responding to Zach. I had been living in isolation for several years now. I was getting out the door more, but what I jokingly referred to as McMan International's world headquarters comprised but a corner of a modest room, one I spent at least ten hours a day laboring in, every day of the week, with only the occasional day off.

Finally, I let Zach know I would be attending. I put out the word in my newsletter, and instantly I was inundated with requests from subscribers who wanted to meet me. One of my subscribers, whom I had already forged an online relationship with, promised to introduce me to the key people in the organization.

Oh, shit! What have I gotten myself into? One part of me was thrilled. The other part of me wanted to crawl into a cave and roll a rock over the entrance.

The evening before traveling to the conference, I go out for a walk. I am nearing the home stretch when I feel myself breaking out in a sweat, my chest constricting, my heart thumping, and my breathing becoming labored. By this time, I know enough about mental illness to realize that a panic attack can mimic a heart attack.

A panic attack is not exactly something you wish for, but when your other choice is cardiac arrest you go with the panic option every time. I take that back. Only 20 months before, when I was suicidally depressed, I would have welcomed a heart attack. Swing low, sweet chariot.

I find a boulder to sit on and await the verdict. After a minute or two, my breathing and all the rest normalizes. Apparently not a heart attack. But I'm not quite ready to test my hypothesis. I sit on that rock another good five minutes before tentatively taking my first baby steps back home.

There is no medical condition to describe what happened to me the next day. I'm in a public rest room at the conference hotel. I do my business and make my exit, only to discover the door won't budge. It appears to be locked from the outside. I grip the knob and attempt to turn it. Nothing. I rattle the door back and forth. Nothing. I feel myself freaking out, about to scream, about to thump against my barrier like a mad man.

Breathe!

I step back. I look around. I spot another door, an open one. I had been trying to exit through the cleaning supplies closet. It's the only time something like that ever happened to me, before or since.

At the conference, I actually succeed in surprising myself. The very first person I talk to there is still my good friend. Once I realize I am in the company of fellow bipolars, people who have walked in my shoes, I am able to relax.

My second day into the conference, I step outside of the hotel. I cross the street, and sit on a bench overlooking the Charles. I am on the Cambridge side of the river, looking into the Boston skyline. But what grabs my eye is the peaceful expanse of water and the sail boats gliding by.

Zach, who I met face-to-face for the first time the day before, strolls over and sits next to me. We talk about this and that, but mostly we share the quiet together. If there's one thing an introvert enjoys more than peace and quiet to himself, it's peace and quiet with another person. I inhale and breathe out slowly. Life is good.

* * *

Fast-forward two years later. The NDMDA—soon to be DBSA—is having its annual conference in Orlando. This time I am looking forward to reconnecting with members of my adopted bipolar tribe and meeting new ones. But there is a major catch: I'm scheduled as one of the closing speakers. Fifteen minutes at the very end.

I will have no choice but to read my talk. What I lack in basic speaking skills, I hope to make up for in literary elegance and soaring prose. But this requires a set of reliably vibrating vocal cords. Despite my misgivings, I feel proud to attach a "Speaker" ribbon to my name tag. I've come a long way. If only I could just walk around with the ribbon without actually having to speak. I do manage to enjoy the conference, but I'm clearly on edge. I make jokes about doing my best Ethel Merman impersonation, but these jokes fall flat.

The evening before the closing session, I feel a cold coming on. I retire early to get some rest. Finally, my big day. The other speakers have finished. Finally, it's my turn. No—first a high school choir has to warble something excruciatingly inspirational. This is getting ridiculous. Now it's my turn. I look out into the room. The closing proceedings have gone on way too long. From my vantage point on stage, I see people fidgeting, checking their watches, anticipating getting to the airport on time. Some of them are already making for the exits.

This was not how I envisioned it. It's a good thing I have a lectern to cower behind. I grip both sides as if I'm scaling Everest's north col, put my head down, and start reading, but in some impossibly high register that only dogs can hear. I do experience a few brief shining moments where I am able to put some passion into my literary passages. Something about enduring pain, hardship, suffering, and humiliation, I recall. We may hate our illness, I say, daring to look my audience in the eye, but we cannot hate what our illness has made of us. It almost manages to come out Kennedy-esque. Somehow, I succeed in closing on a high note.

I gaze out into the room. Half the audience is rising to their feet in applause. I lower my head and scurry off the stage as fast as I can, not wanting to see if the other half follows suit. Besides, those others were only applauding because they felt sorry for me. One of my subscribers runs over and gives me a big hug. I feel my cold overtaking me and exhaustion setting in. I need to make tracks. I need to get out of the room, out of this hotel, out of Orlando, out of Florida. I need the comfort of my own room, to close the door behind me and lie in bed for a week.

* * *

Fast-forward three years later. I'm in Chicago with Tom Wootton, author of *The Bipolar Advantage*. My book, *Living Well with Depression and Bipolar Disorder* has just come out. Tom is giving four talks in the area, and he has offered to mentor me in public speaking. Tom's an accomplished corporate presenter and facilitator. Over the next few days, he gives me the equivalent of a master class.

In nothing flat, I am out from behind the lectern, speaking without notes, actively engaging my audience, talking conversationally. Amazingly, I discover an ability to fly off the script and let loose with some inspired observations that just pop into my head.

It's not like Tom turned me into an accomplished speaker. Nothing close. That takes practice-practice-practice. But what he did for me proved far more significant. Thanks to my series of public trials by ordeal, I soon started noticing something different in my daily life, namely: When I encountered people in routine social settings, I felt far more at ease. I could enjoy the company of others in a way I had never known. The before and after was as spectacular as eye surgery.

However people view me—a delight to have around or a pain in the ass, someone they would like to know better or someone they can't run away from fast enough—they are seeing only one version of "me" on display. They are not seeing the miracle behind the display. Thus, if you find yourself talking to me, you may see the transaction as routine. If I find myself talking to you, though, trust me, from my point of view it's a miracle. Miracles beget miracles. In the last ten years of my life, I'm happy to say, I have been blessed with quite a few.

10

SOUNDING OUT TRAUMA

ALONG with anxiety, trauma is also part and parcel of our stress response. Our best window into this is post-traumatic stress disorder (PTSD).

According to Francine Shapiro, the originator of eye movement desensitization and reprocessing therapy (EMDR) for treating PTSD and trauma, in a 2012 *NY Times* blog, PTSD "occurs when an experience is so disturbing that it disrupts the information processing system of the brain." Memory of the incident is stored, replete with its unexpurgated emotional content. When these memories are triggered by current events, "encoded negative emotions, thoughts and sensations can emerge and color the perception of the present."

The DSM mandates that the individual experience a major trauma, such as rape or a battlefield experience. But Dr Shapiro points out that for many of us, PTSD symptoms can result from less dramatic events, such as hurtful childhood experiences. We have already seen what chronic stress does to two areas of the limbic system fingered in trauma—the hippocampus and the amygdala—plus our cortical regions.

Of all things, Freud's take on how early child experiences can affect present behavior—long ridiculed as obsessing over bad potty training or for blaming your poor mom—is enjoying a comeback.

Basically, my meds got me stable while my lifestyle and coping tools got me healthy. But getting me whole demanded the courage to enter some very dark spaces and embrace a very scared child. But the timing had to be right. If you are feeling emotionally unstable or you don't have your bipolar under control, now is not the time to lift the lid to your early life and start poking around with a stick.

I like to joke that I raised myself and did a rotten job. More seriously, if you were to ask what the biggest challenge of my life was, I would have to say surviving childhood. As kids, even in stable and loving environments, we are always wondering: "Is it safe?" We adapt, we learn to survive, any way we can. For some of us, this involves our brains being rewired for constant danger. Consider a child growing up in poverty. He or she is more likely to have a thinner neocortex than her more affluent counterpart. The frontal cortex has one of the highest rates of receptors for glucocorticoids.

One day I will pen a memoir that includes my growing up. I'm not ready for that, just yet. Back in 1999, though, soon after I was diagnosed with bipolar, in a white heat, I did produce three essays that recounted some childhood experiences not involving my parents. I still have these posted on my *mcmanweb* site. Two of the titles, "When I First Knew I Was Different" and "Alone Against the World," give you a general sense of where I was coming from. Here's the start to "Alone":

It was me, alone, against the world. There was no other way to describe it. It was around age 11 and 12 when I noticed that I was a lot shorter and skinnier than the kids my age. Then they all started sprouting hair in funny places and talking in deep voices in knowing ways, and the realization struck with Biblical force:
My God! I really was different!
It was like those dreams everyone seems to have of turning up in public in just your underwear. If only it were just that. If only the shame and embarrassment were for just one day. If only I could just go home and reach in the closet and slip into my leg and pubic hair the way I could a pair of pants and grow six inches and return to school and blend in and say things like, eat it raw, like I really knew what I was talking about.
No, I was doomed to show up for school in the equivalent of my dream underwear every day for the next three years.

The piece recounts the terror I experienced over having to perform in public a musical composition whose notes totally eluded me. I played trombone in a kiddie dixie band, and we were performing at a well-attended outdoor concert. We pick up my account:

The clarinet player who was the leader of the group gave me the evil eye, as if to say you screw up here and you're a dead man. I walked out onto the outdoor stage like I was going to the gallows, trombone in one hand, music stand in the other—four sheets of music clipped on with clothespins—praying to God we wouldn't have to do an encore, because that fourth piece to me was as decipherable as the Rosetta Stone.

Unaccountably, I nailed the Rosetta Stone piece. It was as if God Almighty had entered my body and played my trombone for me. What came out of my horn had nothing to do with the notes on the page. Let's just say if you're impressed with God's handiwork with fiords and glaciers, wait till you sample his trombone-playing. The crowd went wild. The adult musicians behind us gave us a standing ovation.

Of course, right after that I went back to not being able to play my trombone worth shit, and once more I was alone against the world.

Here's where it gets weird. Fast forward five decades to about two years ago. I'm on a cushion in my living room, practicing my didgeridoo. Until I moved out recently, this was my regular routine. Anyway, somehow I sense the spirit of the clarinet-player in the ether above me. The clarinet-player had grown up to be a world-class bassoonist. So, sensing he was in the vicinity, I asked him to guide me on my didgeridoo.

Why not?

Later, when I googled his name, I discovered he had died a year or so earlier. The fact that I could now have a "relationship" with this clarinet-player, this childhood Scourge of God, was a miracle, one that I owe to my brother. As I stated, I am not ready to write my memoirs, but five years ago or so I was ready to talk to my brother.

Every form of trauma therapy has an element of exposure and desensitization built into it. Namely, you relive past events in a safe setting, to the point where you start feeling comfortable inside your own skin. So it was that over numerous conversations—over my home cooking and beers, listening to Neil Young—both of us felt driven to repeat the same family talking points, over and over. With each repetition, our past lost some of its strange dominion.

Then one day my brother came over, and we talked about sports and music and politics without even mentioning family. We had both turned a corner.

Back in 2002, at the American Psychiatric Association annual meeting in Philadelphia, I heard Charles Nemeroff, then of Emory University, ask this very pertinent question: "Is the biology of depression the biology of early trauma?" Women abused in childhood, Dr Nemeroff explained, end up with a sensitized brain stem, where CRF receptors are to be found in abundance. CRF is a hormone involved in the stress response.

In an earlier study Dr Nemeroff was involved in, depressed women who had experienced sexual or physical abuse as children were put through a battery of public speaking and mental arithmetic tests. These women experienced far greater concentrations of stress hormones than the women in the control groups.

Although the link between past events and present behavior is not fully understood, a picture is emerging of a biologically vulnerable brain being rendered even more vulnerable by the sheer persistence of distant ghosts refusing to be silenced. This makes us sitting ducks for even routine stresses in our daily lives. Our brains become oversensitized to the point where our entire world feels unsafe.

Fifty percent of those diagnosed with bipolar report incidents of childhood trauma. Throw in adult trauma—or simply the stresses of modern life—and we are certainly talking about just about all of us. On top of that, trauma enormously complicates the course of depression and bipolar. This raises the rather obvious point that maybe we should be putting a lot more emphasis on treating the trauma rather than merely throwing meds at our ups and downs.

Then, maybe, our world will be a little less frightening. Then, maybe, once we find it safe to breathe, we can start making traction in our recovery.

The trombone was one of my childhood toys I abandoned as I entered adulthood. It's a familiar story. Life gets in the way. But I also had bad memories associated with that instrument. As much as I loved music, it was easy for me to justify not being actively involved in it. Then, months after I moved to California, in early 2007 the didgeridoo came into my life. Since the didgeridoo is not a western instrument, it didn't carry the negative associations of my trombone. I was free to develop on my own, unburdened by the baggage of my childhood.

Funny thing. Five years ago, at my first didgeridoo gathering in Oregon, I was sitting on the grass, jamming with some of my new didge tribe. A woman came over and apprised me knowingly. "You used to play the trombone," she said. Aha!

Could the didgeridoo, among many other things, have amounted to my own form of exposure and desensitization? A safe instrument for me to express my trombone sensibilities? A safe place to take my music further? Could it be, that when I was ready, my original bandmate would show up? Could it be that I would find his presence comforting?

I have no ready answers, but I love asking the questions.

11

WHEN OUR THINKING GOES WRONG: STRESS AND ATTENTION

ONE of the major stories in bipolar over the past two decades is the growing recognition that the condition is way more than a mood disorder. Part of this involves cognitive difficulties that many of us experience. In a 2004 brain scan study, for instance, remitted bipolar patients performed as well on a simple cognitive task as the healthy controls, but had to activate more brain regions.

As I heard Stephen Strakowski, who we introduced in Chapter Eight and who authored that study, explain in so many words at a conference in 2011, many people with bipolar have to work their brains harder just to stay apace with those around them.

We've already seen what stress can do to cells and circuits and systems. Once again, our old nemesis the amygdala is on the loose, running roughshod over our cortical regions. Turn up the heat and the front end of the brain is fighting a losing battle with the back end. Under pressure, we fare worse than the general population in performing basic cognitive tasks.

Believe it or not, I was relieved to hear this, or at least Dr Strakowski's take on the topic. As he disclosed to his audience, he had originally misinterpreted the results of his own 2004 study. A 2006 article he authored provides an insight. The old brain science, he wrote, is a "form of phrenology" that wrongly attempts to localize specific cognitive and emotional traits to specific portions of the brain.

If we go with the old brain science, it's all too easy to attribute our cognitive and emotional deficits to defective working parts. We are stuck with what we were born with, which is not too encouraging. The new brain science doesn't necessarily dispute this, but it does offer the additional explanation of dysregulated neural networks at the scene of the crime.

The suggestion is that the overload or outage may only be temporary. Perhaps, over time, in the right circumstances, our brains will lay down new wiring. The situation is not hopeless, in other words, though it can seem that way when your immediate situation is rapidly heading south. Thus, imagine yourself in a social setting. This is where we regularly face our most extreme cognitive challenges. Even talking to someone you feel comfortable with may be stressful. But you are holding your own. Then a stranger sidles over and you find yourself struggling. It may take an excruciating extra second or two, for instance, to recall who the George Washington Bridge was named after.

Meanwhile, you are finding it difficult to ignore a million and one things going on in the room. (One of Dr Strakowski's studies found that some individuals with bipolar have problems tuning out background noise.) Now everything seems to be closing in. If someone were to administer a spot IQ test, you might get the part right that involves signing your name.

Then your boss strolls over. Dear God! Just when you most need to be on your cognitive game.

We've all been there. We've all been rendered dumb and dumber. We've all experienced the sensation of our intelligence evaporating like perspiration in a dry desert heat. My first book in this series leads with my own personal account of my brain going AWOL on me during an important meeting and the emotional fallout I had to endure for days after. I also disclosed, though, that I had failed to pay heed to the warning signs. Our limbic system may be a royal pain in the ass, but it serves an extremely useful purpose in alerting us to danger, even if it is prone to frequent false alarms. When my hackles went up, I should have paid closer attention. I should have made some major course corrections.

The lesson to this is simple: If stress affects our intelligence, particularly in social situations, then we need to be intelligent in managing our stress.

ADD/ADHD

Now let's shift our focus to attention. Our best window into this is adult ADD. Nearly one in five individuals with bipolar experience ADD (or ADHD), but all of us (the chronically normal included) have attention problems of some sort. What we seem to be talking about is underpowered cortical circuits, including those involved in executive function. This includes a range of vital cognitive processes such as working memory and attention. The brain may under-focus, bouncing from one distraction to the next, failing to stay on task. Or it may hyperfocus, say on a project or something insignificant, at the expense of awareness of the immediate world or what really needs to be done.

The stories you hear from friends and loved ones are legion. In one instance, as someone reported to me, his ADD friend assured him he was on his way to drive him to his post-operative procedure. The friend didn't turn up. As my informant explained to me, "What could have been more important than getting me to my appointment?"

Key cognitive circuits aren't the only regions experiencing difficulty. Pleasure/reward circuits also experience weak signaling. To compensate, many with ADD take to thrill-seeking, which may include dangerous behavior and substance abuse. The prospect of instant reward—sometimes nothing more than the simple sensation of feeling alive—in turn makes impulse-control highly problematic

On the surface, a lot of this comes across as the type of racing thoughts and over-the-top behaviors of hypomania and mania. But below the hood, different stuff appears to be going on, namely: Whereas the manic brain needs to be slowed down, the ADD brain needs to be speeded up. Individuals with ADD often report living in a mental fog, to the point where they feel ironically depressed. Stimulants, which enhance dopamine-signaling, act to boost their underpowered circuits.

Warning: For those of us with bipolar, stimulants may induce mania.

When these meds do what people hope they will do, chaotic thinking becomes organized, impulse-control normalized. That's the happy ending. The sad one, unfortunately, is all too familiar: Marginalization to the fringes of society. Same old story—like those of us with mood disorders, people with with major attention deficits often prove too hard to live with. Friends and family and colleagues can only take so much.

Okay, the story now gets personal. Several ago, while researching a piece on ADD, I carefully read through the DSM diagnostic criteria for the illness. Much to my surprise, I easily met the threshold. The DSM, though, always needs to be read with extreme skepticism What I noticed was that its exhaustive symptom lists for the condition appeared to describe your classic disruptive kid in the classroom. This, I most assuredly, was not. Rather, I was the prototypical quiet kid – shy, retiring – occasionally coming to life during rare manicky outbursts.

Yes, I could easily tune out my teachers, but who didn't? Moreover, my current ADD-like symptoms could easily be explained by my bipolar and anxiety. Yes, I was prepared to acknowledge, I may be "a little bit ADD." Unlike pregnancy, mental illness is not an all-or-nothing deal. In knowing thyself, we need to be paying close attention to the "little bit of this" and "little bit of that" that may be going on beneath the diagnostic radar.

So, okay, I was willing to concede, I was dealing with a "little bit" of ADD. But I was handling the issue – along with my bipolar and anxiety and tendency to panic – using mindfulness and a whole host of related techniques.

But the issue simply wouldn't go away. For one thing, various author/advocates were bringing the adult version of the illness to public attention. According to them, ADD amongst adults is far more common than once thought. Moreover, it doesn't necessarily manifest as your classic disruptive kid in the classroom.

So it was that I found myself staying as a guest in a friend's house. An urgent business matter came up. She observed my comically panicky behavior. "I have the papers somewhere in this bag," I informed her, as if everything were normal.

But my frustration was evident. Paperwork is my nemesis, organization an impossible dream. Along one vital area of human function, life defeats me every time.

Over the next few days, my friend was able to carefully observe me in action. When the time was right, she busted me. She, too, contended with ADD, she let me know. It takes one to spot one. She asked me a few questions. One of them had to do with math and algebra.

Well, I always tuned that stuff out, I let her know. It was all blah-blah-blah to me. Instead of focusing on my work, I doodled. I got pretty good at it, so good that in no time I was taken seriously as a cartoonist.

Too bad about the math. As I am wont to joke to friends, I liked algebra so much I did it twice. How I became a financial journalist many years later, I can only ascribe to some karmic anomaly.

My friend followed up with questions on how I worked on my projects, big and small. I proudly informed her how I was able to tune out the world around me to devote myself a hundred percent to getting the job done.

"At the expense of getting other things done?" she queried.

Uh, yes, I replied. I could see where this was headed.

"For a lot of people, ADD is about performing the task immediately in front of you," she let me know. "You forget about the dishes in the sink or other things that need to be done." Such as putting important documents in the right place.

77

Or it may be the reverse: You focus on the dishes in the sink or something trivial at the expense of your project-or, for that matter, to show up to drive your friend to his post-operative procedure. Either way, you are a victim of the moment, stuck inside whatever chunk of your world that just happened to land inside your field of attention.

This is entirely different than the distractability (together with memory issues) of Dory the fish in *Finding Nemo* and *Finding Dory*, though, for many people, that is a prominent feature of ADD.

Either way – under-focused or hyperfocused – we pay a steep price.

So, here I was, talking to my friend, feeling a major epiphany in the works. Resistance was futile. A "know thyself" breakthrough was beginning to resonate in my bones. My moment of truth had arrived.

It may turn out that I am still only "a little bit ADD." But, in the blink of one almighty personal revelation, that little bit most unequivocally increased in scope by at least one order of magnitude. One one hand, the thought that I may have one more full-blown psychiatric diagnosis to contend with is enough to send me into depression. It's like every step of the way, my brain is conspiring against me.

On the other, I feel a sense of empowerment. Thanks to my friend, I have identified a significant aspect of what may be holding me back, call it whatever you want. Now, I can roll up my sleeves and get to work. Life is a work-in-progress. We learn as we go along.

One day, I will be able to write on ADD with the same insight I bring to bipolar. I'm a long way from that. But I do feel confident in urging that if you have, or suspect you have, bipolar, to ask to be screened for ADD, whether you think the diagnosis applies to you or not.

An actual diagnosis will require a lot more than just a screening, but a screening will give you and your therapist something to work with.

One final twist ...

Someone I knew quite well a decade or so ago—let's call him Jim—constantly amused those around him as sort of multitasking wonder. Typically, you would find him in a chair, TV on, talking on the phone to one person, carrying on email exchanges via his ubiquitous laptop with another two or three, buying a book on Amazon that his ADD won't let him read, and having a face-to-face conversation with whomever was in the room. Plus something going on the stove or documents being printed, and so on.

Jim would assert that this was his "ADD advantage." Indeed, had Jim been fortunate enough to have been born back in the days of hunter-gathers, he may have been held in highest regard for his preternatural abilities to keep track of so many things at once, like a mother keeping tabs on her kids while performing a million household chores. In Jim's case, these abilities would have made him a natural leader on any hunting expedition.

Or it could be that he would have been eaten by a tiger while he was over-focused on the lint in his navel.

Sure, Jim made a show of doing five or more things at once, but from my observations this came at an unacceptable price. Studies indicate that jumping from task to task—distraction to distraction—effectively wipes your working memory clean, before whatever was there can be locked and loaded into your long-term memory.

This helps explain those "refrigerator moments" that happen to all of us. You know, you find yourself staring into the interior of the fridge, unable to recall the purpose of your mission. In all likelihood, you didn't "forget." Rather, you got distracted along the way, say by a text message or the sight of dirty dishes in the sink. In this case, we're talking about an attention issue rather than a memory problem, though the result can be the same.

Now imagine someone like Jim, jumping from distraction to distraction, deluding himself into thinking he is accomplishing five things at once. His days may appear full, but what do his yesterdays look like? Is he staring through disconnected fragments into empty space?

Ironically, with the advent of the smart phone and texting and the explosion in social media, Jim comes across as almost normal. You might actually call him a pioneer. Add to that the fact that our public places are brimming with distractions. What evil mind, for instance, came up with the notion that we needed to be watching TV as we pumped our own gas?

Christ, in some places, I can't even take a shit in peace.

It could be that kids growing up in this environment will succeed in radically rewiring their brains for effective multitasking. Who knows? I'm guessing instead that we are setting ourselves for the greatest dumbing down of our species since evolution took a wrong turn at agriculture 12,000 years ago. We will be discussing that particular catastrophe in later chapters. In the meantime, we've all turned into versions of Jim. Ten years ago, when someone like Jim came up in a conversation, we would just shake our heads knowingly and laugh. Now, we're too busy clicking "Like" to someone's cat photo on Facebook while carrying on a conversation while ordering pizza and watching Netflix. One tiny decade. That's all it took.

12

WHEN OUR THINKING GOES WRONG: THE PLEASURE AND OBSESSION TRAP

Let's be clear: Pleasure serves a vital evolutionary purpose. If it weren't built into our reproductive wiring, none of us would be here. Not only that: If some kind of virus were to take the joy out of sex for every individual on the planet, well the good news would be no more worries about overpopulation. Yes, we would be sure to find the rare dutiful drudge mating with another dutiful drudge, but the result, I submit, would hardly be called human.

Pleasure is no evolutionary icing on the cake. As well as providing a key incentive for us to reproduce, it also powers our work ethic. That satisfactory dopamine rush from completing a tough assignment or mastering a new skill? Chalk it up to pleasure and its attendant rewards. We now have the will to roll up our sleeves and get back to work. We practically salivate in anticipation of our future pleasure and reward. Anticipation of pleasure, in turn, produces its own pleasure. For lack of a better term, call it motivation. Our lives now have meaning and purpose.

In case you're wondering what life without pleasure would be like, simply ask yourself the name of the condition whose core symptom is loss of pleasure, and, by extension, lack of motivation. That's right, it's called major depression, the most disabling illness on the planet, a form of death-in-life that takes down people in their prime. Even its less severe manifestations can strip your world of sound and color and all that brings simple enjoyment.

Who wants to live in a world like that? Far too many, tragically, opt out.

Perhaps the best way to understand how pleasure drives us is to take a look at the famous Stanford "Marshmallow" Experiment. Back in the late sixties and early seventies, researchers presented preschoolers with the choice of one marshmallow (or other treat) now, or two later. The researcher then left the room, leaving the marshmallow on the table. In follow-up studies done in the eighties and nineties, the researchers found that the kids who succeeded in holding out for two treats tended to have higher SAT scores and other favorable quality of life measures.

The authors of these studies view their results in the context of delayed gratification and willpower. This involves self-control, the ability to override one's habitual and automatic reactions in a voluntary and purposeful manner. Not surprisingly, a 2011 brain scan study on some of the original participants found the high delayers exhibited more cortical activation. But the brain scans also revealed something else going on: The low delayers showed more activity in the midbrain's ventral striatum, which houses the nucleus accumbens, part of the brain's pleasure circuitry.

To add a bit of context, the other major player in the circuitry is the ventral tegmental area (VTA) perched above the brain stem. The system runs on dopamine, the VTA is a virtual dopamine fuel pump.

What we seem to be looking at is that sensitivity to pleasure/reward can undermine our best efforts to govern our lives. And – wouldn't you know it? – cognitive psychology is showing that bipolar patients are sitting ducks. For instance, one study involving a card-sorting task found that symptom-free bipolar patients were more responsive to small monetary awards than the control subjects. Another study found that bipolar patients engaged in gambling tasks took greater risks than their more "normal" counterparts.

Risk-taking, of course, is a positive trait. Our culture celebrates its daredevil entrepreneurs and athletes, along with those other rare breeds with the courage to buck the odds and blaze their own trails, come hell or high water.

But we also need to be mindful of the downside. One engaging and colorful character I became familiar with was addicted to alcohol and crystal meth and gambling. He lived from one cheap thrill to the next, and this included hustling for nickels when he could have been earning honest dimes. His father, by contrast, was a former Navy pilot who became a successful real estate wheeler and dealer. Same type of dopamine-driven risk-taking, pleasure-seeking behavior as his son, we can argue, only far more constructively directed.

In the meantime, we have longitudinal studies—the type that track subjects over time—showing that pleasure/reward sensitivity is a major predictor of the course of the bipolar. Last but not least, researchers can point to brain scans showing that encouragement can light up our pleasure/reward circuitry while criticism shuts it down.

We're a long way from separating out cause from effect. A good performance review, for instance, may trigger an over-response in pleasure/reward, which may in turn set us up for hypomania or mania. Or it could be that an underlying depression deadens our response.

Recall our earlier discussions on how an over-reactive amygdala has a way of triggering fear. Pair fear with pleasure and we now have a workable description for bipolar, one we can see as a condition characterized by our acute sensitivity to our environment, with stress and fear coming at us one way and pleasure and reward the other.

Let's go back to our marshmallow experiment. Part of me says I would have been one of those kids reaching for the treat. I even like to joke about it. But another part of me says I might have remained in my chair, frozen in fear, not daring to incur the wrath of any lurking adult.

Fear one way, pleasure the other – even when our frontal lobes are fully online, how we decide and act at any given time often comes down to the stronger emotion in the deck.

Thus far, we have viewed fear in a negative light, the end product of our limbic circuitry overreacting to our environment. But our amygdala and its supporting cast are there for a reason. Thanks to our fears, we are alert and engaged. We exercise sound judgment. We don't run with scissors, we don't drink the Kool-Aid, we look before we leap.

Now let's tap into our unconscious, where fear and pleasure engage in an ongoing and mutually cooperative tug of war. In his 2009 book, *How We Decide*, science-writer Jonah Lehrer takes us back to the closing seconds of the 2002 Super Bowl. The New England Patriots have the ball deep in their own territory, and the Rams defense is expecting a young and inexperienced Tom Brady to pass. In the split seconds he has at his disposal, there is no time for him to make a considered decision.

Crunch-time. Brady takes the snap. His primary receiver is tightly covered. He feels a twinge of fear. His secondary target is also covered. Again, a negative feeling. Brady needs to get rid of the ball in a hurry. He spots his third receiver streaking across the center of the field. According to Lehrer: "When Brady looks at the target, his usual fear is replaced by a subtle burst of positive emotion. ... He lets the ball fly."

Think back to the last time you changed lanes in freeway traffic. Pretty much the same thing. Now think about the last time you voted and what went into your decision. Hint: If you claim you made a rational choice based on carefully sifting through the evidence backed by a lifetime of insight and wisdom, you are in an acute state of monumental delusion.

During the 2004 Presidential campaign, researchers at Emory University scanned the brains of an equal number of partisan Republicans and Democrats as they were presented with contradictory statements from the two candidates, George W Bush and John Kerry. The participants in the study, predictably, found ways to rationalize their own candidate's lapses in judgment while condemning those of the opponent.

No big deal, right? Here's where it gets interesting. Once the rationalization was made, the ventral striatum, where the nucleus accumbens is located, lit up. Thus, when our study subjects were presented with a justification that fit their particular belief system, they experienced a subtle surge of pleasure.

The pleasure they felt, in other words, validated their biases, gave them permission to be jerks.

This is no isolated study. In the last two decades, testing subjects across all manner of settings, a flood of research has poured in supporting the notion that rational thinking is a myth, that we essentially think with our emotions. Fear drives us one way, pleasure another. This doesn't diminish us in any way. It's simply how we roll. We're not infallible. We're, uh – human.

Presumably, we are meant to learn as we go along. That's more or less how the warranty to our frontal grey matter reads (but try getting a refund). We learn from past mistakes. We make the necessary course corrections. But there is a major catch: Pleasure has a perverse way of keeping us stuck in our suspect and bad behaviors. We feel good doing stupid stuff. We feel just as good rationalizing it, better perhaps. Where is the motivation to change?

The sooner we recognize this glitch in our operating system, the better. Negotiating this wholly strange planet we find ourselves stuck on is difficult enough without contending with misleading feedback from our brain's pleasure circuits. Heaven help that we end up like our Uncle Shithead, you know, the one who ruins everyone's Thanksgiving. The one I'm thinking of we referred to as Uncle Bigot. Literally, his face would light up every time he used a racial or ethnic or sexual preference slur. He literally lived for embarrassing himself.

Fortunately, I suspect, he never got too many invitations to experience this odd pleasure in public. His loss, our gain.

It doesn't stop there. There are far too many people in our lives who can't seem to help but create drama, pick fights, show off, and otherwise make an ass of themselves. Then there are those in thrall to their bad habits and guilty pleasures and crackpot beliefs. On and on it goes. The causes are many and complex and will probably forever remain a mystery to us, but at the end of the day, when all is said and done, you are certain to find a nucleus accumbens at the scene of the crime, gorging, or at least nibbling, on dopamine.

It's always going to be easy to feel good about being a prisoner of your old beliefs, ones that no longer serve you well. Making the changes you need to be making, by contrast, is much easier said than done. Too often, the cure is a healthy dose of misery, the consequences of our disastrous choices.

Alas, if life were meant to be easy, there would be a smartphone app for it.

* * *

We now transition to our obsessions and compulsions. This may seem like a long leap from pleasure. Bear with me. I will connect the dots.

Obsessive-complusive disorder (OCD) conjures up the image of the "neat-freak" who is phobic about things out of place or the wacky eccentric who feels compelled to perform silly rituals such as not stepping on the cracks in the sidewalk. The most famous fictional example is the TV detective Monk. The show couldn't resist playing up the humorous side of Monk's strange behaviors, but it also sympathetically portrayed him as a man who was uneasily misunderstood, who couldn't accomplish even the simplest of tasks without a paid assistant, who was medically unfit to return to his former job as a police detective, and who was unable to enter into a loving relationship.

The most famous OCD sufferer in history, the inventor Nikola Tesla, fit a similar pattern. On the comic side, he was fixated on the number three and its multiples, which, among many other things, involved walking a certain number of steps before entering his hotel. His room was on the 33rd floor. But he also could not bring himself to touch women, which meant he remained celibate his entire life.

Welcome to OCD hell. On a neural level, are talking about a failure in the brain to screen out certain thoughts. We see an enviable and benign manifestation of this when we become attached to a romantic partner. Call it love, if you want, but also recognize the obsession that goes into its making. Also have regard to the heartbreak we feel when our love goes unrequited. And also be mindful of all the things that can go wrong when an innocent romantic obsession builds into a destructive fury.

84

Meanwhile, in some types of depression, we find a dangerous tendency to over-ruminate on our worries and various dark thoughts. What both conditions have in common—romantic attraction and ruminating depressions—is a lack of serotonin to certain brain circuits. Significantly, the first drug that specifically targeted serotonin, Luvox, was approved in the US back in the eighties for OCD rather than depression.

Clinical trials for antidepressants typically test depressed patients en masse, with no regard for key differences in their respective clinical conditions. I'm guessing the ones who best respond to a serotonin-enhancing antidepressant are the over-ruminators in the bunch, the ones whose condition most resemble OCD. But until a drug company actually targets this specific population (which they won't), we are totally in the dark.

The overlap goes further. In extremely rare cases involving individuals whose previous treatments have failed them, both conditions have been successfully treated by surgically inserting an electric lead (a procedure known as deep brain stimulation or DBS) into the cingulate cortex in the mid-brain. Switching on the lead has the effect of disrupting the intrusive thoughts. The same surgery is well-established for movement disorders such as Huntington's, and the parallels are well worth noting. In Huntington's, for instance, we have a failure in the brain in not screening out certain movement impulses, equivalent to the OCD brain unable to screen out certain thoughts.

Now imagine fiction's most famous obsessive, Captain Ahab. A great white whale is one hell of a huge thought to have trapped inside your head. But something more is going on than just the mental image of a large aquatic mammal. Ahab is also bent on exacting revenge, and these ruminations, of all things, will dispatch dopamine to his pleasure/reward circuits. Or, more accurately, circuits responsible for anticipating the pleasure/reward, which will initiate its own form of pleasure/reward. Heaven help when the interplay between obsessive thought and pleasure/reward compels us to do something not in our best-interest.

See? I told you I would connect the dots.

Okay, we know how empty our lives would be without pleasure. But when things don't go according to plan, pleasure/reward only winds up feeding our whale. Poor Ahab. Things didn't work out too well for him in the end.

Now substitute that whale for someone who has treated you badly. You're justified in your thinking, of course, but still—this is one huge whale to be carrying around. Now throw stress—with all its attendant cognitive and social challenges—into the equation, and here you are, obsessing on your boss while checking eBay for harpoons, when suddenly the man who is ruining your life walks into the room. How are you going to react?

Several years ago, a casual acquaintance of mine disclosed to me his anger issues. He let me know that when he was put on a certain serotonin-enhancing med, the anger went away. But for good reason, he didn't want to become dependent on a "happy pill." But was the med really a happy pill? Did it really clear up the anger? Or was something significant taking place further back along the chain of causation? Was the serotonin, albeit temporarily, actually sealing off years of resentful thoughts—obsessions—that had somehow become lodged deep inside certain neural circuits? Could it be that once the obsessions disappeared his anger no longer had anything to feed on?

Who knows? But I trust that you are beginning to appreciate the sheer complexity of human behavior. To add another layer of complexity to the topic, imagine our obsessive thoughts engaged in an unchoreographed pas de deux with our numerous personality issues. We will be exploring our negative tendencies in full in the next two chapters. In the course of that discussion, I ask you to contemplate all the many disasters we are courting when the worst inside us—say a tendency to demonize a person for some imagined insult—finds a juicy pleasure-driven obsession or two to chew on.

Let's get into it ...

13

DIAGNOSIS: POISONALITY

IN an article on my *mcmanweb* site that I have since retired, I led off with this fictitious example:

Rewind a bunch of years ago. Bill treats his mom to a cruise.

Fast forward to the present. An aunt is being laid to rest. Bill's mom happens to mention the cruise to her daughter. As the casket is carried out, the daughter pulls her other brother aside and says in a voice quivering with rage, one that carries into the distant pews, "She really knows how to push my buttons!"

Everyone would agree that the daughter's behavior is highly inappropriate, but is it consistent with a personality disorder?

Or could it have been a heat-of-the-moment thing? Let's suppose the daughter—call her Amy—had been especially close to her aunt. Suppose for two days, in her state of distress, she has been enduring a steady stream of sugar-coated insults from a mother she can barely stand. Then mom makes a seemingly innocuous comment that sets her off.

Understandable, right? Normal even, you can say. Hell, who hasn't let loose in similar situations? Okay, now compare that to an encounter I had recently. I am fictionalizing details here. The potato salad, though, is real:

I was having lunch with someone I had met not long before—let's call her Pamela—someone who lived nearby who identified as having bipolar disorder. As one who lives with the same illness, one that takes no prisoners, it's vital that I cultivate relationships with people that I can check in with from time to time. We had met briefly a few times before, and now we were getting to know each other. We were both feeling calm and relaxed. The sun cast a warm glow on our outdoor table, and we quickly opened up.

Pamela related to me a recent text exchange with her next-door neighbor. She had been soliciting advice about a personal issue, and the neighbor responded with her take on the situation. Then the neighbor added: "But I'm no expert."

"Go to hell!" my new acquaintance texted back, stinging like a wasp.

Frozen luncheon tableau. One individual looking across the table to me for validation, the other one—me—fork in his potato salad, eyes averted, a study in suspended animation.

You can make a very strong case that the sum total of my millions of years of evolution anticipated this exact moment. Our smaller brains from way way back may have proved sufficient for protecting ourselves from predators, but our much larger ones from 200,000 years ago serve a singularly useful purpose in protecting us from each other. Consider:

Was my luncheon companion about to erupt like my fictional Amy? Was she going to let loose on me like she did with her neighbor? Or were there extenuating circumstances? I was going to need every neuron at my disposal to figure this out. Let's see ...

Pamela is now making a short speech about how people are supposed to be genuine, say what they mean, not equivocate, and all that.

I sense my hackles standing on end. Her story doesn't "feel" right. The front end of my brain is now on the case, scanning my knowledge banks, pulling up personal memories, synthesizing information, fashioning a response.

The words, "borderline personality disorder," followed by three exclamation points flash before me. That extra punctuation is not superfluous. I have had very unfortunate encounters with people I later discovered were living with this condition. Let's investigate ...

Borderline Personality Disorder

In my first book in this series, I characterized borderline as a "failure of normal." This separates it from bipolar, where our "normal" tends to represent a mostly symptom-free safe harbor. In bipolar, our manic and depressive episodes are defined by behavior "uncharacteristic" of our true normal. In borderline, by contrast, we can make a case that an individual at both their best and worst is all too in character with their true "normal," that the whole package—the good, the bad, and the ugly—is firmly rooted in that person's core personality.

Mind you, we bipolars are no angels. An individual with bipolar is as equally capable of telling a person to go to hell for no good reason. This is likely to arise out of an agitated version of depression or hypomania. The difference, though—assuming our bipolar individual is an otherwise decent person—is he or she, upon return to normal, is likely to be mortified by his or her behavior. If we're not looking for a crack in the floor to shrink through to hide our shame, we are reaching out to repair the damage we caused.

By the way, if you happen to be a friend or loved one, please do not let your bipolar associate off the hook so lightly. Abuse is abuse. You need to stand up for yourself.

So here I was, fork still stuck in my potato salad, listening to my acquaintance justify her behavior in a perfectly conversational tone, days after the event. Something was clearly wrong with this picture. I'm not about to declare after-the-fact justifications as the new litmus test for borderline personality disorder, but it does offer us a valuable insight into a range of personality "disorders" that the DSM lumps together under the heading of "Cluster B" to indicate those with dramatic, emotional, and erratic tendencies. As well as borderline, these include sociopathy (or psychopathy), narcissism, and histrionic (which we will disregard, for now).

Forget labels, for the time being. If we need to find a commonality across these conditions (excluding histrionic), it's that our attempts to establish any kind of meaningful relationship with certain people are frustrated by their obdurate refusal to take ownership for their actions.

In other contexts, I have made reference to the "asshole diagnosis." I'm not being flippant, here. We waste far too much of our lives on people whose only regard is for themselves, who only wind up hurting us. Often we get sucked in by their superficial charm before they reveal their true colors, leaving us feeling violated and abused. For people with our diagnosis, with our built-in vulnerabilities, the effects can be catastrophic.

What are we dealing with, here? That is the fundamental question. Friend or foe?

I am no fan of the DSM, but I do urge you to read the symptom lists of its four "Cluster B specials" (including histrionic). As a thought experiment, you might want to select one or two or three items from each list and shake and bake to come up with your own special breed of problem individual. In effect, we are building our own diagnosis. Here's mine. Call it whatever you want:

- Identity disturbance.
- Very strong sense of entitlement.
- Deceitfulness.
- Uncomfortable in situations in which he or she is not the center of attention.
- Inappropriate, intense anger.
- Emotional instability.
- Lack of remorse.
- Lacks empathy.

Lest we get smug: In all likelihood, at least one or two of the symptoms on my list, in some measure, applies to you personally. This is why putting together your own list is such a useful exercise. As well as alerting you to what you need to be looking out for in others, you just may hit upon an insight or two into what is holding you back.

If only it were just bipolar. Always, always, there is other stuff going on.

So here I was, mere minutes before, reaching out to a woman named Pamela, looking to forge a human connection. We are social animals, after all. Our brains were built to be around people. But they were also built to keep us out of danger. Pamela may or may not have met the diagnostic criteria for borderline. That was not my concern. What mattered to me, simply, was that I was seeing very clear signs of inappropriate anger and emotional instability, and a possible lack of empathy. She had already, by her own admission, lashed out at one innocent bystander. I had no intention of being her next victim.

At the same time, though, I could spare her a kind thought. Let's assume she was contending with borderline. The experts tell us that people with this condition are extremely fragile, lacking a strong sense of self, often having experienced intense trauma in their lives, at the mercy of the stress-driven vagaries of genes and environment.

Because the condition is built into the personality, there is no pill for it, and heaven help if there ever were. Heaven help if we had meds to change something as intrinsic as our own identity. Pamela's core will remain fairly constant throughout her life. She can change, but—like all of us—she will be accomplishing this against the tidal tug of all those mysterious forces that shape who she actually is.

90

Over time, Pamela will hit upon new adaptations, ones that better serve her than her old ones. Eventually, she will learn that a "go to hell" response is something you reserve for those who actually have it coming.

In the meantime, there is no running, no hiding. If this were an episode of the *Twilight Zone*, a judge from another dimension might have sentenced my luncheon companion to a life sentence inside her own brain. I, for one, cannot think of a worse fate. Tragically, far too many with the borderline diagnosis feel the same way. Like those of us with bipolar, these individuals are just as likely to opt for what they see as the only way out. But as worthy as the Pamela's of this world are to our sympathy and understanding, always—always—we need to be protecting ourselves. No exceptions.

Happy to say, in my case, I was able to extract the fork from my potato salad without incident. As for Pamela, she has her work cut out for her. You may want to wish her luck.

Antisocial Personality Disorder

"Predator," is the only term to describe your classic sociopath, with us as their prey. In these people, as opposed to those with borderline, we see a much stronger sense of identity, together with an often disconcerting lack of emotion, which comes in handy when squashing your best friend like a bug.

The ones we succeed in locking up and throwing away the key tend to comprise a variant unable to reign in their impulses or who occupy the bottom rungs of the socio-economic ladder. The smarter and more privileged find ways of rising to the top of the heap, as CEOs and political leaders and so on, such are the social advantages of having bug-squashing capabilities built into your DNA. True sociopaths comprise but a tiny portion of the population, but their influence is enormous. Their values—such as they are—permeate our culture and influence how we think and feel. We will be discussing this in full in Part Four of this book. In the meantime, simply consider how just one symptom attributed to sociopathy can skew a person's personality: "Lack of remorse."

Narcissistic Personality Disorder

This diagnosis is much misunderstood and hotly contested, so much so that the first draft of the DSM-5 removed it entirely. My view is the condition is all too real, but it defies our clinical attempts to pin it down.

Both my parents exhibited narcissistic tendencies in abundance. Being a kid, I mistook their behavioral excesses for normal. Not surprisingly, this led to my attracting partners with similar qualities, ones who wasted no time in assigning me fringe planet status in their own wholly me-centric universes.

You think I would have learned by now, but no—very recently, a so-called dear friend summarily banished me to a particularly remote region of her social galaxy. This happened days after I underwent bypass surgery.

"Lacks empathy," reads one of the symptoms from my problem person list. "Strong sense of entitlement," reads another. As well as being classic narcissist traits, these symptoms would also look good on any sociopath's resume. The key difference, though, is how the individual with narcissism relates to us. We are not prey. We are simply bit players in their play.

We may not recognize this arrangement until a personal crisis hits us, when we find ourselves in time of need. This is when we expect our close ones to rally around us. The last thing we're expecting from someone particularly close to us is to be hit hard with displays of cruel indifference. The experts even have a name for it—the narcissistic cold shoulder. In my time of need, my so-called dear friend flicked me off like a flea. I never saw it coming. We never do.

This is a good time to bring up "gaslighting." The term comes from the classic Alfred Hitchcock movie, *Gaslight*. As part of the mind games the villain played on his victim, he would surreptitiously dim the gaslights, then, when confronted, deny any change in illumination. The victim thus began to question her own perception of events, and, ultimately, her sanity.

Gaslighting is a favored ploy across the Cluster B disorders (possibly excluding histrionic): The perpetrator denies events, or at least the victim's interpretation of events, to the point where roles may be reversed – the victim feels like she did something wrong, the perpetrator becomes the victim.

A version of this happened to me in my friendship breakup. I was the one recovering from heart surgery, but somehow I wasn't paying enough attention to her. Crazy thing, I almost started to believe it.

Incidentally, as a thought experiment, you might want to ask yourself how someone with either borderline, sociopathic, or narcissistic tendencies would break off a friendship. There are no right or wrong answers, here. You can find mine in my insect metaphors: Sting like a wasp, squash like a bug, flick off like a flea.

The damage can be long-lasting and traumatic. We may never recover. Hence the need to protect ourselves. Always, always.

Now for a major disclaimer: It is all too easy to dehumanize people who give us a hard time. Think carefully before you reach for a diagnostic label. In the case of my friend, there may have been other reasons to explain her hurtful behavior. What I feel safe to say is her actions were entirely consistent with those of someone with narcissistic tendencies.

And the mandatory kind thought: According to the experts, people with pronounced narcissistic tendencies often act the way they do to compensate for their own insecurities. The grandstanding boorish braggart, for instance, may deep down feel like a hopeless loser. In short, your standard garden variety narcissist is not a happy person.

I like to think that my former friend possesses the degree of insight to learn from her past experiences and work at changing her behavior, and thus arrive at a deeper level of satisfaction in her life. The catch is that any narcissistic tendencies she may have will only militate against this type of insight. She is very successful in her business, one that places her in the center of a well-populated universe, with no shortage of admirers. In short, she is living the narcissist dream. So where is the incentive for her to change? Is there a better reality for her than the dream she has built for herself? That is something for her to figure out.

Histrionic Personality Disorder

This was another personality disorder the DSM-5 was originally looking to deep-six, and for perfectly valid reasons. As opposed to the malevolent characteristics of its far more notorious Cluster B mates, it is fair to say that histrionic personality disorder falls under the category of "mostly harmless."

This is not to diminish the distress certain people with histrionic characteristics may face. It's just that lumping them with the Jack the Rippers of this world seems a trifle unfair.

The diagnosis raises the immediate stereotype of the corset-encased Victorian woman who faints at the slightest provocation, unable to handle the demands of life. Indeed, these women represented Freud's bread and butter. Back then, the condition was referred to as hysteria—dating back to antiquity—and was assumed to be a biologically based disease peculiar to women.

No doubt there was a lot of it going around in Freud's day. These tended to be your educated and intelligent young women with dreams of their own, being forced into strictly regulated lives as obedient wives and mothers. Their emotional distress tended to manifest as all manner of physical symptoms.

Freud seemed to identify with their plight, but being the male patriarch he was, living in the age he did, he attributed their condition to a classic failure of adaptation. Thus, rather than validate his women patients and give them the confidence to dare to seek lives on their own terms, he saw his job as helping them adjust to their socially assigned life sentences.

And Freud being Freud, he couldn't resist folding frustrated libido into the equation.

Crazy thing, maybe Freud was right about this. The term, hysteria, was still au curant in the 1950s and 60s, when it was employed to describe the stereotype of your classic 1950s neurotic and sexually repressed housewife. But, following the cultural revolutions of the 60s and 70s, and with it a wider range of career and sexual outlets for women, perhaps the condition had run its course.

This would be a classic case of changing the environment to eradicate an illness, like draining a swamp to wipe out malaria.

But the diagnosis remained, albeit with a new label - histrionic—and with emphasis on a new suite of symptoms, ones that raised a new stereotype, that of the emotionally insecure and attention-seeking drama queen. Not exactly the type of individual who seems to specialize in making our lives miserable.

Drive us a bit crazy, at times, to be sure, but hardly one to avoid at any cost.

In the new iteration of the diagnosis, it's easily to imagine that engaging and daffy talk show celebrity from the 50s and 60s, Zsa Zsa Gabor, perhaps the first individual to fashion a career based on being famous for being famous. Typically, she lit up the room, greeting her admirers with exaggerated affectations, addressing everyone within earshot as "Dahlink."

To someone with histrionic tendencies, literally everyone is "Dahlink," and therein lies this individual's Achilles heel. In its modern incarnation, the diagnosis places emphasis on the individual's lack of ability to differentiate between casual relationships and intimate ones. "Dahlink" could be the doorman. It could also be your fiance.

This is where the real problems start. Reading a deep relationship into a shallow one, for instance, is certain to set one up for heartbreak and disappointment. It's happened to most of us at one time or another, histrionic or not. And how did you feel when the inevitable letdown occurred? Depressed?

It goes further: If you are deluding yourself into believing that a casual acquaintance is, say, the love of your life, or that someone you barely know is your dearest friend, then your interactions with him or her are sure to come across as highly inappropriate. Fortunately for women, they are cut a lot of slack by being referred to as "flirtatious," a term that inevitably arises in any discussion about histrionic. Change genders, though, and we have the classic case of your boorish male pig. Either way, flirtatious or boorish, the boom gets lowered. You find yourself out in the cold – again.

Ms Gabor, incidentally died in 2016 at the age of 99. She had nine husbands. As she famously quipped: "I want a man who is kind and understanding. Is that too much to ask of a millionaire?"

14

DIAGNOSIS: POISONALITY—A CLOSER LOOK

LET'S return to our fictional Amy from the previous chapter, the one who made a scene in church at her dear aunt's funeral. It's tempting to try to place her in a neat diagnostic bucket, such as borderline personality disorder, but, in our messy real world, symptoms tend to spill together like paint from upended cans, resulting in their own quirky colorations. Indeed, the people in charge of personality disorders for the DSM-5 wanted to phase out diagnostic categories altogether in favor of a truer-to-life "dimensional" system.

Sort of modular, like putting together IKEA furniture. Build your own diagnosis. The old guard, though, put up such a stink that the old categorical regime remained intact, as if we hadn't learned a thing in two decades.

A dimensional system also tests for severity. To return to our paint analogy, all the tints may be in the mix, but in highly diluted form. Since "highly diluted" would accurately describe just about all of the population, we can hardly pathologize "normal." Nevertheless, we do need to cultivate a special regard for how just one tint, however seemingly insignificant, may profoundly color our behavior. This is how we will be looking at Amy, as someone perfectly normal, but with some traits that bear close scrutiny. Let's begin by checking out her personal history:

Age 49. Masters degree from Princeton. Policy analyst with a state government agency. Has held this position for ten years. Has a number of investments and is able to holiday abroad regularly. Has lived in the same condo over the same time period and regularly entertains friends there. Has a reputation as an excellent hostess and a good cook.

So far, so good. Pretty impressive, actually. Moving on ...

Married once, no kids, divorced two years later. No long-term relationships since. Has told mom 15 years running that she is six months from submitting her novel manuscript. Her friends call it the next Wuthering Heights. *Has been on diets since her teens. Now she appears to have given up. Says she will join an exercise program once she has submitted her novel ...*

Hmm. Worth investigating further. Why don't we start with her next *Wuthering Heights?* The manuscript, she lets everyone know, steams with hot sex, which she broadly hints is autobiographical. But then we learn her last fling was twenty years ago.

Okay, loving relationships aren't easy. But at least she has friends. But hold on. They seem to be a revolving bunch, drawn in by her hostess skills but driven away by unfortunate misunderstandings over her next *Wuthering Heights.* Now she's telling her new friends that she's going to have her own show on the Food Network. After all, she's a good friend of Rachel Ray's, and she wouldn't be saying that if it weren't true, right?

Wait! Something doesn't add up. How can someone this—uh—singular have held down a high-responsibility job in state government for the last ten years? Funny you should ask. On further investigation, we find our dear Amy is a glorified data entry clerk who shares a cubicle with someone she hasn't talked to in two years. Because she has the good fortune to belong to a public service union, no one is about to sack her. Her masters degree from Princeton, by the way, is more like a certificate from Western Princeton Tech in South Dakota.

The only thing about Amy that is not in dispute is her age. For the last five years, she has been adamant about being age 49. Her OK Cupid profile, though, lists her as 45.

Amy, Amy, Amy. But before we start judging her, how much of her do you recognize in you? If we assume that our Amy is essentially normal, not that much different than your standard-issue human, including you—you, and me—then we need to more closely examine ourselves. But this is way easier said than done. For instance, ask a random sample of people to rate their driving abilities and everyone will tell you that they are at least above average.

You will get a similar response when you ask people to rate their intelligence. Yet, in both instances, simple math dictates that half the people in each sample must be below average. The phenomenon is known as the Dunning-Kruger Effect, after the two Cornell psychologists who who came up with their great Aha! As I tend to phrase it: The stupid and incompetent are essentially too stupid and incompetent to recognize their own stupidity and incompetence.

By contrast, the better we are at something, the more we tend to entertain self-doubts. If our self-doubts don't cripple us a la Hamlet, they serve as the driving force in our own personal and professional improvement. Brilliant surgeons in effect self-doubt their way to ever greater brilliance.

To freely extend Dunning-Kruger, we can argue that we're often far too delusional to know we're delusional. Our personal delusions invariably constitute our best defense against unpleasant realities. When things go right in our lives, we tend to take credit. When they go wrong, we may attribute the outcome to bad luck or blame others. There is a technical term for these people—well-adjusted.

Scientific fact: The optimists in our midst—delusional as they may be—are happier, healthier, and they live longer.

Who, after all, wants to be a self-doubting realist?

In one recent well-publicized experiment, researchers openly rigged a series of Monopoly games in favor of one group of participants. Advantages included twice as much money in the bank or additional rewards for passing Go. Within minutes, the "privileged" players became more aggressive in their behavior. Later, they attributed their inevitable success to their brilliant board strategies.

Now we start getting into the downside of our personal delusions. Once we have bought into them, it becomes all too easy to rationalize our outrageous behavior, the type not meant to win friends and influence people, the type you see popping up on those Cluster B symptom lists.

But—and this sounds crazy—we need our personal delusions. If you have any doubts about this, try to recall what happened to you when they failed you, when you, in effect, suffered from a massive bout of reality. Chances are you became seriously depressed.

Here, we need to rethink depression. Conventional wisdom posits that our distorted negative thinking plays a major role in our depressions. The most common talking therapy for depression—cognitive behavioral therapy —is based on helping us remove those distortions. As it turns out, though, pessimists and a lot of us with depression display preternaturally realistic tendencies. We see through our own and other people's delusions, and predictably we're not all too happy.

When our delusions collapse, when our defenses break down, when we have no choice but to look reality straight in the eye, here at long last we may find ourselves experiencing the true "beast" of depression. Can we handle the truth? Let's return to Amy. ...

The party's over. The last guest has left. The dishes are stacked in the dishwasher. Amy pours herself a wine, flops on the couch, and contemplates her evening. Her guests loved her, of course, and she thinks they were wonderful, too, and her shrimp dish was a smash.

Perhaps it's best to leave Amy marinating in her own fantasy world. In the meantime, we need to keep reminding ourselves: This chapter is as much about us as it is about her. No us vs them. It's about us, plain us.

Having said that, we do need to remind ourselves that we are literally surrounded by the likes of Amy. The classic DSM sociopath or narcissist or someone with borderline may be a relatively rare breed, but bits and pieces of their symptoms are widely dispersed throughout the population.

"Inappropriate, intense anger," for instance, can be found everywhere. It's difficult enough for us to understand the strange customs of the denizens who occupy the world of "normal" without having to contend with some of their Cluster B add-ons, as well. Especially if these same individuals feel entitled by their sense of normal.

Know thyself, know others. Whether in protecting ourselves or in moving our recovery forward, understanding is our first step, anticipating what may go wrong the next. Taking preventive action follows. Last but not least—cultivating the ability to forgive. At the very least, we need to learn to laugh at our own follies. Let's close by returning to where we started, back with Amy, live at her aunt's memorial service ...

It's later in the day, and the gathering has reconvened in the church rec hall. Now Amy is making nice with the family. She tells her mother how good she looks and fusses appropriately over her three nieces. Okay, reaching for that second piece of cake after she just informed people of her just-diagnosed diabetic condition may have raised eyebrows, but even cynical cousin Paula is flattered to hear they must "do lunch" sometime soon.

"I'm flying out to see a client tomorrow," she lets everyone know, as if to apologize for her early exit. We now learn that she has a consulting business on the side. Only this "client" of hers is actually a Ponzi artist out to separate her from her personal fortune.

That's right, the personal fortune. Amy's been dropping hints for more than a year. Something about her investment advisor getting her into South African gold futures. Or maybe it was Ukrainian oil. But the joke is on the Ponzi artist. Little does he know that the personal fortune he has heard Amy refer to involves the film rights to her next *Wuthering Heights*, the one that has been in a state of near-completion for 15 years, the one that Steven Spielberg will be shooting any day now.

And I think to myself, what a wonderful world ...

15

ADDICTIONS: MYTH, REALITY, AND WHO KNOWS WHAT

I COULD fill up several books on what I do not know. Instead, I will confine myself to a few insights I have picked up along the way. Let's start with a major aha! moment that hit me seven or eight years ago.

I was having dinner with a group of individuals involved in NAMI (National Alliance on Mental Illness). NAMI was founded in the late seventies by parents with kids with schizophrenia. Decades later these individuals still form the core of the organization's membership.

Inevitably, the conversation turned to their kids. The stories I heard would break your heart. These were people who had experienced the dreaded three o'clock in the morning phone call more than once, and were living in mortal fear of the next one. Hospitalizations, homelessness, run-ins with the law, on and on.

Naturally, I assumed these parents were talking about schizophrenia. Then one happened to mention bipolar, then another, then another. Bipolar? Something didn't sound right. Then the penny dropped.

You guessed it. It wasn't "just bipolar" I was hearing about. Thanks to drug and alcohol abuse in the mix, life's degree of difficulty for all parties concerned went from "challenging" to "just about impossible."

How bad is it? Again, at first I thought these parents were talking about schizophrenia. That's how bad it is.

According to numerous population studies dating back to the 1990s, six in ten people with bipolar have experienced alcohol or substance abuse or dependence at some time in their lives. To be clear, the numbers relating to abusing drugs and alcohol any one time are much lower, but we're still talking about frightening statistics. Walk into any bipolar support group and the people there talk about "self-medicating." Walk into an AA or NA meeting, on the other hand, and you will hear people talk about their insatiable "cravings." You don't need to be a brain scientist to figure out that self-medication has a way of turning into a craving. But it helps to have a brain scientist or two give us a reliable starting point.

As I heard Nora Volkow, head of the National Institute on Drug Abuse, describe it at a 2011 conference, "all drugs of abuse increase activity in the nucleus accumbens."

Ah, the pleasure circuitry. That glass of wine at happy hour may bring out the best in you. Before you know it, you're having two. But it's not quite that simple: Dr Volkow was quick to add that stress is also an active player.

This summons up our celebrated "short allele" having to do with stress-induced depression. No surprise, this gene variation has also been fingered in alcoholism. Same glass of wine (or two), but this time you're using it as an anti-anxiety med. It is no coincidence that alcohol and benzodiazepines such as lorazepam work on the same neurotransmitter system, GABA.

Alcohol (ethanol) and benzo molecules mimic GABA neurotransmitters. Now we suddenly have fake GABA flooding the brain, doing the same stuff the real GABA does (only with far more spectacular effects). When they lock on to GABA receptors, they essentially send the same message to the neuron as the real GABA does by telling it to chill.

One result is that the neuron fires off fewer glutamate neurotransmitters, which are all about exciting the neuron. When things go right, the two systems—GABA and glutamate—work in harmony, helping keep our moods and energy levels in balance. But who wants balance if your current reality happens to overwhelm you? Or what if out-of-balance is your new normal?

It's not just about the GABA and the glutamate. Somewhere down the line, we have the release of dopamine into the ventral striatum, where we find the nucleus accumbens. Recall that pleasure plays a crucial role in motivation. We're going to want to experience that same pleasure again, and our brains will reward us accordingly. This is perfectly normal. People drink alcohol all the time without getting addicted. But what if things start veering out of control?

Let's bring Dr Volkow back into the picture, but with a different beverage, coffee. Check out the title of this study that she was involved in: "Caffeine increases striatal dopamine D2/D3 receptor availability in the human brain."

Coffee, good to the last drop, in other words.

Like alcohol, the caffeine molecule mimics an actual neurotransmitter, in this case adenosine, and locks onto a corresponding neural receptor. Only this time, something different happens: Instead of sending an adenosine-type message to the neuron – in this case, telling it to relax and go to sleep – the caffeine molecule blocks out any incoming adenosine neurotransmitters. Adenosine cannot complete its mission. We remain wakeful or become alert.

Something different is also going on with the dopamine connection. According to the study Dr Volkow was involved in, instead of dopamine flooding into the striatum, we have the creation of more dopamine receptors in this location. This would give the naturally occurring dopamine already there more opportunities to bind to the neuron.

An indirect dopamine-enhancing effect, in other words, but with all the difference in the world. We can savor our coffee without the loss of control that characterizes addiction.

With drugs of abuse, on the other hand, we have a decrease—not increase— in dopamine receptors. The brain, in essence, is shielding itself against the onslaught of drug-induced dopamine neurotransmitters. But when things return to normal, there are few places for our naturally occurring dopamine to land. Striatal neurons are literally screaming for the stuff.

Thus we have the conditions for a craving, which sets the scene for an addiction. We're not taking the drug because we "like" it, but because we "need" it. We've become prisoners to our messed up pleasure circuitry.

Looking at it this way, the active chemicals in addictive drugs—ethanol, opioids, methamphetamines, nicotine, and so on—form only part of the addiction picture. Always, always, we need to pay regard to the dopamine effect at the end of the line. Dr Volkow is very insistent on that.

Let's switch from drugs to gambling, food, and sex. All three have been recognized as addictions. The first two have their own DSM and ICD codes. The latter has an ICD code, as well, and would have received DSM recognition had the task force in charge of the latest edition not rejected the recommendation of its own work group.

Nothing wrong with any of these activities, mind you, but when your passion turns into an insatiable need, when you lose your sense of control, Houston, we have a problem.

If we truly want to get creative, we can even bring my late Uncle Bigot back into the picture. No, we're not about to immortalize his behavior with his own ICD code. Simply—for teaching purposes—have regard for the fact that the guy couldn't seem to help himself. It was as if his nucleus accumbens stood up and applauded every time he let loose with the N-word, K-word, or Q-word.

Consider one particularly bad habit a good many people are hooked on, one that triggers excruciating emotional and physical pain as one engages in the activity, the type we associate with various forms of self-torture. With repeated use, users may find themselves crippled to the point of requiring major surgery – feet, knees, back, any part of the body responsible for keeping us upright and mobile. The damage can be long-lasting and even permanent.

Any activity this painful and potentially disabling, of course, requires one hell of a justification, and its users don't disappoint. Here they turn into poets and spiritual teachers. They describe a strange state of mind that comes across as either an ultimate Zen paradox or extraordinary load of self-justifying bullshit, depending on point of view. Just when the pain can't get any worse, they will tell you, just when the brain is about to raise the white flag, an extraordinary wave of bliss overtakes them. They take wing and fly. Their spirits soar. They enter a new realm free of physical and spiritual gravity.

What they are experiencing, of course, is runner's high. It's as if the body, under certain conditions, were producing its own recreational drugs. Indeed, this is certainly the case.

Of all things, we were born to run. Sometime soon after we climbed out of trees and settled into life on the savannah, our distant ancestors developed their own unique locomotion system ideally suited for ranging long distances. At close range, though, our new adaptation proved comically deficient. Unless you're Usain Bolt, for instance, even a hippo can chase us down. But turn feet and yards into miles, and the game changes. The hunted becomes the hunter.

In his illuminating 2009 book, *Born to Run: A Hidden Tribe, Superathletes, and the Greatest Race the World Has Never Seen*, journalist Christopher McDougall goes back in time to conjure up whole tribes of our distant ancestors on the hunt—women and children, too—running constantly, days on end, keeping pace with their quarry, wearing them down until they eventually reduced even the proudest and mightiest in their midst to panting and pathetic quivering balls of fur.

Over the long haul, long legs rule, two per owner. Not any old long legs, mind you—long legs with buttocks to keep the rest of us upright. Our close chimp cousins lack this feature. Another secret weapon: sweat glands, the perfect cooling system for tooling across the open savannah.

And, of course, our massive brains to tell our long legs—not to mention other people's long legs—where to go.

Our ancient awesomeness is on display in Mexico's remote Copper Canyon. There, the reclusive Tarahumara Indians routinely run a hundred miles or more at fast speeds without incurring the type of injuries that plague western runners. Mr McDougall attributes running injuries to the modern cushioned running shoe, which encourages landing heel-first, which is apparently not natural.

According to Mr McDougall, we need to land on the balls and toes of our feet and drop slightly to our heels, as if running barefoot across the lawn. This is how the Tarahumara Indians do it, with only thin rubber sandals as protection.

Sooner or later, westerners had to get into the act, running impossible distances in extreme locations: There is the Badwater Ultramarathon that takes place over a 135-mile course in Death Valley in the heat of summer. We also have the Leadville Trail 100 (as in miles) that traverses the Colorado Rockies in oxygen-scarce altitudes that range between 9,200–12,620 feet. At least they don't run it in the dead of winter.

Mr McDougall's point is that thanks to our ancient survival adaptations, long-distance running, even at inconceivable distances, is perfectly normal.

From this, it's easy to see how nature plugged pleasure/reward into the effort. The common explanation for runner's high is that sustained physical exercise produces "pleasure hormones" known as endorphins, which can best be described as natural morphine. Natural morphine would also ease the physical pain produced by the wear and tear of intense physical activity. The catch is that endorphins have a hell of a time crossing the blood-brain barrier, so maybe we need to find other candidates.

One would be THC, the same chemical found in cannabis. A recent study found that runners—at least mice who run—have higher levels of the stuff in their blood than normal.

So, whether we have endorphins or THC or something else—or maybe all of them together—some mind-altering drug produced inside the body is blissing out our jogging public. The only question is how the dopamine connection fits into all this. Sure enough, a recent study found higher levels of dopamine in the ventral tegmental area in the brains of mouse joggers. As you recall, the VTA forms part of our pleasure circuitry. Where we find a loaded VTA eager to pitch, we are likely to find an eager nucleus accumbens, ready to catch.

Thus, we have the preconditions for a true addiction. It's not that every runner is chemically hooked. Far from it. It's just that no one who sticks with the activity only does it for the fresh air and exercise. And, no, we're not talking about weirdos or freaks. Only in a world far removed from our ancient roots would some people even think like that. Perhaps we need to change our world.

This brings environment back into the picture. To get an appreciation for this, let's return to the world of alcohol and drug addiction.

Recall those anti-drug PSAs from the 80s. One of them shows a lab rat helping itself to one cocaine food pellet after another until it falls to the floor of its cage, dead. A voice-over informs us that this is the fate of nine in 10 lab rats. Cocaine, says the voice-over "can do the same thing to you."

Powerful message, but is it accurate? Or would any reasonable rat confined to a cage go for the cocaine, in a sense opt for the only release available? What if you changed the little guy's environment? Say built a rat park for him and his buddies, with the animals free to choose between regular water and drug-laced water. Back in the late 70s, Bruce Alexander of Simon Fraser University did just that. Voila! Happy rats with real options. Now they could truly just say no to drugs. They did. No matter what, these well-adjusted rats couldn't get hooked.

Not only that, Dr Alexander found that a group of drug-addicted rats he had confined to cages recovered when moved into Rat Park.

Dr Alexander published his findings in 1978, where, until fairly recently, they were totally ignored. You can even say suppressed. That's what happens when your hard facts go up against the War on Drugs establishment, which by this time had coopted just about the entire research community.

The story is told in Johann Hari's eye-opening 2015 book, *Chasing The Scream: The First And Last Days of the War on Drugs*. According to the author, in an article in *The Huffington Post*:

Professor Alexander argues this discovery is a profound challenge both to the right-wing view that addiction is a moral failing caused by too much hedonistic partying, and the liberal view that addiction is a disease taking place in a chemically hijacked brain. In fact, he argues, addiction is an adaptation. It's not you. It's your cage.

If you want human examples, Mr Hari has them. For instance, of the large population of heroin-addicted soldiers returning home from Vietnam in the 60s and 70s, against all expectations, 95 percent kicked the habit. They had lives to return to.

Meanwhile, 15 years or so ago, Portugal had the good sense to acknowledge that its war on drugs had failed. Instead, they decriminalized drugs and redirected the money used on enforcement into treatment and housing and subsidized jobs. Says Mr Hari: "I watched as [drug-users] are helped, in warm and welcoming clinics, to learn how to reconnect with their feelings, after years of trauma and stunning them into silence with drugs."

Since decriminalization, injecting drug use in Portugal is down by 50 percent.

Sad to say, in the US and elsewhere, instead of getting rid of the cage, we build cages. It's almost as if the people who invented the war on drugs were part of some evil genius Kremlin master plan designed to destabilize the economies of the entire western world. Vladimir Putin must be laughing his ass off.

By now, you have probably figured out that the best cure to any addition —chemical or otherwise—is to change your environment. As I heard the legendary psychiatric geneticist Kenneth Kendler explain at the 2009 American Psychiatric Association Annual Meeting in San Francisco, the environment may neutralize genes. For instance, if you make it difficult for a kid to obtain alcohol, then certain alcoholism vulnerability genes have less chance to kick in.

The next day, alcoholism expert Mark Shuckit of UCSD, went into greater detail. A lot of his research has to do with a certain genetic vulnerability to alcoholism called "low level of response." These are individuals who need to have a lot more drinks to feel the same intoxicating or pleasurable effect as their peers, ones who freely recall how back in the day they could drink everyone under the table.

Consider the paradox here: The ones most inclined to feel the effects of alcohol are the ones most likely to be satisfied with a small amount. They might stop drinking after two beers. The one least inclined, though, may feel the need to keep drinking, say 10 beers.

This, Dr Schuckit went on to say, sets up an unfortunate scenario: You start hanging out with heavy drinkers, who, in turn, expect you to engage in heavy drinking.

That old genes-environment two-step, again. In this case, you change your environment by changing your friends. You might argue that AA accomplishes just that. Never mind for now the Big Book and the 12 steps. What you have going for you is a new social and support network consisting of people who don't drink. Something similar happens when drug addicts join faith communities. They're now around people with a sense of purpose to their lives, who have something to live for.

Slowly but surely, we dare to imagine better lives for ourselves, we learn to dismantle our own cages. But then we come to the most challenging cage of all, the one inside our own heads, our own special version of the Sylvia Plath bell jar. How do you escape from that?

I tend to describe bipolar as a condition where we think and feel wider and deeper than the general population. Everything about our thinking and feeling is more intense and less predictable. If we get stressed and anxious, we really get stressed and anxious. If we feel that life is hopeless, we really feel life is hopeless. If we feel on top of the world, we really feel on top of the world.

A reader of mine once referred to our illness as the "really really's." So what happens when the really really's either suddenly overwhelms us or slowly wears us down? How do we cope? How do we adapt?

Recall those NAMI parents I was talking to. Their kids are pushing at least two rocks uphill. They'll need all the help they can get.

16

SOCIALLY CLUELESS

EVERYONE who has tried online dating has their own memorable horror story. Here's mine ...

My OK Cupid feed turned up a "100% match." I knew better, of course. But even if she were only a 97, I was still looking at an attractive woman with professional qualifications and artistic sensibilities. I thought nothing of the dog she was posing with.

I contacted her—let's call her Mary Ellen—and we arranged to meet at a certain beach for walking dogs, not too far from Sea World in San Diego. It was a long drive in from rural East County, but, hey, when we're talking about the possible next love of your life, what's a little extra distance? We would get to talk while walking her dog. At the very least, I would enjoy a morning at the beach.

On the way down, Mary Ellen called to inform me that a certain puppy tutorial was taking place on the beach, and I could join her there, if I liked. OK.

A little back story: The dog she had posed with had died six months earlier and she was breaking in a puppy.

San Diego has a great beach for people who like to walk their dogs. This was not that beach. Instead, I drove into some kind of dark grit wasteland that had once been used by the military. So now, instead of just having to worry about dog poop, I now had to consider the possibility of setting off some abandoned explosive device.

I parked my car and found my way to the outdoor puppy school. There, I picked out Mary Ellen. I greeted her, but she paid me scant notice. She was, after all, attending puppy school. I could wait.

In due course, puppy school wrapped up, and now we had a chance to talk. We headed for a particularly poop-rich section of shoreline. As an added bonus, the beach was under siege from squadrons of recreational jet-skiers.

"What kind of dog is that?" Mary Ellen asked. Clearly, she wasn't talking to me. The guy at the other end of this particular leash let her know that it was a mixed terrier-spaniel with a bit of husky. Or it could have been a great dane with a generous helping of wiener schnitzel. Really, all matters relating to the realm of dog entirely elude me.

"What kind of dog is that?" Mary Ellen was onto her next target. Then her next. And her next. And next. All this time, she totally ignored me. Okay, maybe I wasn't her type, but, like, hello?

Then she came upon one dog-owning couple with their precious one chasing a tennis ball off the leash. Mary Ellen picked up the ball and held onto it, engaging the owners in dog talk. She kept the ball in her hand.

She kept talking, and talking. She didn't relinquish the ball.

And talking. The ball stayed embedded in her hand. The dog couple looked my way, as if pleading with me to do something. The dog looked my way, pleading for me to do something.

You do something, I wanted to reply. Transport me out of here and drop me down in a place where I feel loved and wanted. Military boot camp, federal prison, lunch with Rotarians. Anywhere but here. Maybe I could make a mad dash through the poop and undetonated ammo and hijack a jet-ski and speed off to freedom. Maybe they could make a *Die Hard* movie out of it.

In due course, Mary Ellen decided she needed to change her footwear. We pulled away from the dog traffic and sat down. At last, we had a chance to talk. I opened my mouth to speak, but she was no longer there. To my utter amazement, she had bolted, footwear in hand, chasing down someone she vaguely knew from way way back.

That was the final straw. But instead of running for dear life, I politely waited. And waited. Ten minutes passed. When she finally deigned to rejoin me, I informed her we had a major problem. In hindsight, I could have been more circumspect and come up with some face-saving pretext for leaving right now. Needing to return a library book comes to mind. So does setting aside every third Saturday for cleaning my didgeridoos. But I had suffered long enough. I deserved the satisfaction of an explanation.

I was totally unprepared for her answer. "What?" She replied. "You're not allowed to talk to people you meet?"

How could I explain? I tried, but that only prompted her to pile on more justifications, each one more ridiculous than the last, all of them having something to do with the fact that she was perfectly within her rights to pay absolutely no attention to me. In fact, she informed me, she was under the impression that I had driven all this way just to watch her in action with her dog.

Huh?

Finally, she told me that she had ADHD. This didn't sound right. "Uh, have you ever been treated for ADHD?" I asked.

No, she admitted. It was a long slow death march back to our cars.

Back home, I informed my good friend and mother confessor, Louise, living in LA, what happened. She reacted as if I had been born yesterday. "Haven't you ever heard of dog people?" she asked.

"I think you have the wrong mammal," I let her know. "I know all about crazy cat ladies. But these are dogs we're talking about. You know, man's best friend. My brother owned a dog ..."

"But he had a family," Louise informed me. "It's different with single people." She was familiar with her fair share of them. In her case, these were women who had built their whole lives around their four-legged companions, who hadn't dated in years, whose only other social contact was with other dog-owners.

"Kind of like crazy cat ladies?" I queried. "Only, you know, with dogs?"

Sort of like that, she affirmed. When you cut yourself off from humanity, she let me know, the first thing to go is your people skills.

Okay, she had a point. No more women posing with their dogs. Instead, I would go for the type of gal who got along well with her probation officer and spelled tomato with an "e." What could possibly go wrong?

Two or so years later, I found myself shooting a series of videos with my awesome bipolar buddy, Maggie Reese. Those of you who read my first book in this series will recall that I devoted the better part of a chapter to Maggie, including a photo of her with her dog, Murphy. In our videos, Maggie brings out the best in me. The camera shows me far more at ease than my introversion and social anxiety would normally allow.

As for Maggie, the camera reveals a lively and engaged and wickedly funny woman.

Our videos were done on the fly. One of us would pick a topic, and we'd just start talking, no script. Over two four-hour sessions a week apart, we succeeded in shooting 26 videos, each averaging about 17 minutes. Our first round of filming covered such topics as music, exercise, and handling sensory overload. Then we took a lunch break. When we finished, Maggie suggested that we do one about pets. So we recruited Murphy and let the camera roll.

Owning pets or just being around animals, of course, is an enormous benefit to one's mental health, and we had no shortage of things to talk about. In Maggie's presence, Mary Ellen was the very last thing on my mind. Only much later—like about five minutes ago—did I realize that we had a tale of two dog-owners, one socially clueless, the other an absolute joy to be around.

It wouldn't be appropriate, of course, to contrast Maggie's virtues with Mary Ellen's deficits. But it is fair to point out that when Maggie and I see each other, she takes the trouble to ask about how I've been, and then to express interest when I tell her. It's amazing how many people get that vital part of of human interaction wrong.

The model of the socially clueless individual, it goes without saying, is the character of Sheldon Cooper in *The Big Bang Theory*. Sheldon is the archetype of the brilliant geek who can't figure out people. Not that he wants to. Except when they happen to serve his needs, he regards his fellow humans as unworthy of his attention. Social nuances totally elude him. All this results in comically inappropriate behavior. Sample dialogue:

Amy's Mom: It's nice to meet you too, Sheldon. I honestly didn't believe Amy when she told me she had a boyfriend.
Sheldon: I assure you, I am quite real and I'm having regular intercourse with your daughter.

Add to that no end of behavioral quirks and we have Sheldon comfortably situated in the more functional end of the autism spectrum. For good reason, Sheldon's autism never comes up in the show. This is comedy, after all, which deals in exaggeration and absurdity. We don't want to create wrong impressions.

I bring up autism here simply for instructional purposes. By acquainting ourselves with the condition, we stand to gain greater insight into the plethora of daily social challenges we face in our lives.

Memoirs such as Temple Grandin's 1995 *Thinking in Pictures: My Life with Autism* allow us a little bit of a peek inside, though our understanding remains woefully incomplete. The little we do know about autism points to neural anomalies in language processing and pattern recognition, plus a host of other factors. Heaven help if your brain is not wired to pick up the fine shadings in human speech or facial expressions. A simple hello may be within your field of comprehension, but a more complex one dipped in sarcasm or irony may sail strait over your head.

But try to imagine a world where everyone is the same. People who perceive the world differently than others, if given a chance, tend to have a lot to offer. No surprise, the autism community has introduced us to "neurodiversity," the idea that society needs to better accommodate those who think and act a bit outside the social norm. "Different," in other words, is not to be equated with "deficient." Indeed, in many situations, different can represent both a clear advantage and a boon to society. This is one of the main themes of this book. Guess where I drew my inspiration from.

But we always need to recognize that, however blessedly different we may be, our success as social animals depends on our ability to adapt, and this includes fitting in with those around us. This also emerges as a major theme in this book. Missing vital social cues carries an unbearably high personal cost. We've already seen this in many contexts, from many different sources—from mania, from depression, from introversion, from stress and anxiety, from social isolation, from attentional deficits, from the complexities of our unique personal make-ups, from our pleasure circuitry playing tricks on us, on and on and on.

I was fortunate enough to stumble into conditional deliverance. This occurred at the beginning of 2004, when I moved to central New Jersey. I had no sooner settled in than I discovered that a DBSA group in the area was setting up a group in nearby Princeton. Next thing, with a bit of nudging, I was the founding facilitator.

For improving your social skills—or, for that matter, anything in life—there is nothing like total immersion in an activity that is way outside your own comfort zone. We already saw this with my social anxiety and public speaking. Here, I needed to learn to attune myself to the needs of anywhere from a dozen to two dozen people in the room.

Over time, I became proficient in picking up subtle signs and signals—like a young Mark Twain spotting a tell-tale ripple on an otherwise calm Mississippi—and to calibrate my responses accordingly. At first, I thought I was simply becoming a better facilitator. Only gradually did I realize I was acquiring some invaluable social skills, ones I probably should have learned back in the fifth grade. It's never too late.

In Part Five of this book, we will discuss how our sensitivity to our social environment can make us particularly adept in reading people and social situations. It's an amazing gift, one that borders on psychic, but one that can further alienate us from humanity if we neglect to learn a few basic social rules of the road. It starts with walking a mile in someone's shoes, perhaps along a poop-strewn beach. Tread carefully, live well ...

17

THE EGO AND FEAR EQUATION

IN INVESTIGATING the types of behavior that may be holding us back, it is helpful to look deep inside ourselves, to the private spaces of our ego and fears.

Let's begin with the proposition that a strong and healthy ego is vital to good mental health. By the same token, though, various universal teachings advance the idea of our ego as something that gets in the way. Basically, if we're not careful, over-investing in our misplaced sense of self dooms us into repeating our past mistakes. One outcome is that we find ourselves prisoners in lives seemingly not of our choosing.

The antidote, according to this line of thinking, is to dissolve our ego boundaries in a way that permits an opening up of possibilities, including a new awareness of ourselves and our world. That awareness may be as profound as a spiritual awakening or as mundane as an enhanced ability to enjoy food.

In earth-shaking, Rumi-inspiring love-making at its best, for instance, we lose ourselves in the experience. We cede control, we merge into our partner. If it's music we're talking about, we're looking to cultivate a direct experience with the performance, unfiltered by our cultural conceits. I think all of us intrinsically get that. We learn to pity those stuck in their own egos, in their hopelessly limited lives. If they would only just learn to get over themselves.

But shedding ego is not for wimps. Our tendency is to cling to what we are familiar with, even if it's the source of all our troubles. The unfamiliar, after all, is a frightening place. So now we have the making of a destructive dynamic where ego and fear feed off each other, giving rise to all manner of things that can go wrong.

Here's the crazy part. That precious ego we are holding onto is but an illusion. What we regard as the seat of our conscious is nothing more than a collection of incomplete memories at any given moment, many of them fuzzy and inaccurate. As for the beliefs we hold dear, most of them would not stand up to hard cold reason. In getting through our lives, inconvenient facts are the enemy.

To be frankly cynical, we might characterize ourselves as a collection of delusions masquerading as an identity. Heaven help should someone presume to challenge whatever the hell passes for that precious "me" we so tenaciously cling to. Or God forbid should someone close to us open us to the possibility of exchanging one small delusion for one that may serve us better. No, it's easier to keep lying to ourselves. We may laugh at our fictional Amy from an earlier chapter, but my model for her character happened to be someone I knew very well, or actually didn't know at all—my father.

The man he wanted me to believe he was—that he so sincerely wanted to believe he was—was that of a successful businessman, a mover and shaker, a civic leader and bon vivant, with a sexy wife and model family. On one level, he could live that illusion: A Depression-era boy of Irish ancestry made good, he had successfully made the post-War jump into the middle-class, with a secure white-collar position in a large public utility company. Indeed, he had succeeded beyond his wildest dreams. Had he only left it at that.

But no, despite his lack of education and limited abilities, early on he convinced himself he was a man going places. By the time he turned 40, though, it was clear he couldn't live up to the high standards of his carefully crafted illusion. Depression set in and he started drinking heavily. Within a few short years, he found himself back in the same position he had held earlier in his career—technically a manager in charge of his local office, but in reality a glorified administrator.

Starting out, he had been a young man with a dream, eager to make a good impression. Now he was a has-been, taking up space, having been weighed and measured and found wanting. In any other universe, he would have been out on the street, forced to take a good hard look at himself. This is the situation nearly all of us with our diagnosis find ourselves in. In some cases, it's our illness that disrupts our careers. In others, it's our careers, or the effects of being downsized, that awaken our dormant vulnerabilities. Typically, it's a combination of both.

So here we are, our life pulled out from under us, facing some brutal choices. Our environment has turned on us. For whatever reasons, our old delusions are no longer serving us. Which part of our egos do we shed? Which do we keep? It's as if we have been ordered to stick a sharp object in our eyeball. What on earth can possibly be more frightening than performing surgery on your own identity?

Not surprisingly, this is not the sort of thing we do on our own initiative. I'm guessing my father would have had a much happier and far more fulfilling life had he simply dropped the pretense that he was a successful businessman. But he had no incentive. He was not out on the street. He still had what amounted to his job for life, and he still had his family. In these circumstances, it made sense that he stick with the only self he knew. But to maintain that monumental delusion, he had to expend all his psychic energy building an elaborate array of supporting ones.

It was around this time he started serving on some local boards and commissions. Now he talked about how the local political establishment wanted him to run for mayor, a position he professed to have no interest in, but a topic he kept coming back to. Meanwhile, he would let slip that the idiots in the head office of the company he worked for didn't know how to use his special talents. These were the type of people to which he assigned various versions of the term, "ass." As in wise-ass, smart-ass, and horse's ass.

Now these people were suddenly everywhere. Heaven help if their facts got in the way of his penetrating philosophical brilliance. "Don't be a (wise, smart, horse's) ass!" he would scold his kids. "Balls!" he would yell out in a drunken fury when all other arguments failed him.

"The girls" in his local office were much more accommodating. They laughed at his jokes. They validated his pearls of wisdom. I assume he did "work" at the office, but that never came up in the course of family conversation. More likely, we would hear about some character he ran into at his local "club," where he seemed to spend most of his time. From what I gather, "clubs" serve the convenient purpose of providing cover for the respectable classes to lay siege to their livers. Back in my father's day, apparently, doing this on company time was standard practice.

Any retelling of his encounters at his club, needless to say, only served to buttress his status as a big man about town. Oddly enough, he had the press clippings to prove it. His various board and commission duties, not to mention company ones, required him to show up in public settings, with flashbulbs popping. In this context, his talk about running for mayor bore a slight ring of credibility.

But, then, in the next instant, he would talk of pulling up stakes to open a burger joint on Cape Cod.

Something about Cape Cod or the rugged Maine coast brought out a certain bohemian side in him. There was an artist or writer inside him yearning to get out. I first noticed it as a boy of six as I accompanied him on an evening stroll on Peak's Island in Maine. We sat on a boulder together, just staring out at the luminous waves exploding against the rocks. Sometimes kids have the wisdom of elders. I could feel it, feel it deep, how he seemed to connect to an essential part of his soul. He wasn't trying to be who he was pretending to be. He could just be. Both of us, father and son, just being—together.

Two summers later, I tagged along with him as he traveled along the beaches and lighthouses of Cape Cod, sketch pad and oil paints in hand. I was content to just watch him paint, observe him as he journeyed deep into his interior world, connecting to a part of him that was off-limits to him back home. It could have been that same summer that we were staying up late one night in our cabin, candles glowing, radio on, as we listened live to the very first Newport Jazz Festival.

This was the father I knew and loved, who trusted me enough to take me into his world. It could be opening day at Fenway Park with Ted Williams stepping up to the plate. It could be standing out in the cold to well past midnight, warming ourselves to fires set in metal trash cans, waiting for Senator John F Kennedy to make a campaign appearance. It could be stopping frozen in my tracks at an art gallery, viewing my first Van Gogh.

This was also the father I lost. Bizarre behavior piled on top of bizarre behavior. His kids now existed solely to serve his delusions, and heaven help if we let him down. His anger, always a problem, now erupted at the slightest imaginary provocation. His drinking—combined with possible stimulant abuse—turned his brain to mush. Then the physical problems set in. He could no longer be the man he was pretending to be. He had no idea how to be any other kind of man. He could only hold on to the one he knew, at any cost. He paid one hell of a price.

Somehow, he managed to hold on till age 74. For the sake of my mother and his surviving sisters, I managed to deliver a glowing eulogy. The father I started losing at around age 12 was one I could truly mourn. At various times in my presentation, the words got stuck in my mouth and

I had to pause to catch my breath. As a dutiful son, I gave it my best effort. I included a little vignette about how I took him by the arm as he walked out the door of his home for the very last time, on his way to a hospital procedure he wouldn't survive. The two of us, father and son, walking his last steps together.

He seemed to know it. He was ready. At long last, he was able to let go.

This concludes Part Three. On to Part Four ...

PART FOUR

A BRIEF HISTORY OF HUMAN BEHAVIOR

"I tell you, we are here on earth to fart around, and don't let anybody
tell you different."
—Kurt Vonnegut, *A Man Without a Country*

18

200,000 YEARS AGO: SYSTEMS AND HIGHER INTELLIGENCE

WE'RE BACK into our genes-environment narrative, the one that began four billion years ago when molecules organized into replicators and later genes. Our next stop was 500 million years ago, following the Cambrian Explosion and life emerging in new complexity. One of these involved fully developed neurons and primitive neural circuits appearing in sea snails and other creatures.

Then came a fortuitous comet from 65 million years ago that cleared the earth of dinosaurs and opened the way for mammals. In the rat brain, we now see sophisticated neural systems designed to respond to danger.

Then we jumped ahead to three million years ago to "Lucy," an almost-human primate about to evolve a larger brain. Thanks to her already higher intelligence, she not only has to worry about predators and natural disasters, but about fellow members of her species.

The story continues ...

Timeline: The sixth day of creation. Improbably, in the late 1980s, genetic researchers singled out a hypothetical African woman from 200,000 years back who was to become known as "Mitochondrial Eve." It isn't that our Eve is the only woman on earth, or that there weren't other generations before her. Rather, she simply represents our most recent common ancestor, traceable through our mothers and the mothers before her, going back in time to fewer mothers, then fewer still, till at last we only have one. One mother, Eve.

Just her. This bears emphasis. Not the pregnant woman to her right. Not the pregnant woman to her left. Their respective mother-daughter lines were doomed to die out.

Not Eve's own mother, either. She would have represented our second-most recent common ancestor, not our most recent.

Prior to unearthing our hypothetical Eve, the fossil evidence lent credibility to two competing scenarios. The first contends that Homo Sapiens emerged in more than one location, from Homo Erectus populations that had left Africa more than a million years ago, as well as the Erectus populations that stayed behind.

By contrast, the out of Africa theory—supported by our Eve—posits that Homo Sapiens evolved relatively recently from a select Erectus population still in Africa into an even more select Sapien population, and that our ancestry traces back to this new breed of Homo and no other. Moreover, Mitochondrial Eve supports the notion that only a small and perhaps isolated band of Sapiens made the final cut, that the rest of our species was taken out by a some sort natural catastrophe or through sheer attrition.

As for all those Erectus multitudes still around at the time of Eve, ones who had made a successful go of it for an impressive two million years or so, first in Africa and then spreading into the Middle East and Asia, in a relative blink of an eye they would be no more. Only their bones and artifacts would be left behind, not their lineage.

The impression we get is one of Darwinian inevitability, with Eve and her descendants, augmented with a new suite of killer genes, poised to overrun the planet. It is far more instructive, though, to view our common mother as a lot more vulnerable, tenuously clinging to existence, a natural disaster or two from her and her species going extinct.

Anatomically, she is just like us, with an abnormally large brain three times the size of Lucy's, and a third larger than the Erectus line that she and her kin have recently broken away from. The maintenance costs are enormous. Comprising just two percent of her body's mass, her brain accounts for a wildly disproportionate 20 percent of her metabolism. This means she is going to have to devote far greater time and effort to gathering food.

The metabolic demand has also turned her into the Stone Age equivalent of the 98-pound weakling. To compensate for the high operational costs of running a brain, natural selection has slashed the budget on all body mass from the neck down. A chimp can beat the stuffings out of her.

Plus poor Eve must devote years of extra time and effort in raising her slow-to-mature big-brained children. This will necessitate the involvement of an exclusive male partner—or, alternatively, non-exclusive males and females living communally—willing to take on some of the child-rearing load.

Nevertheless, these Darwinian hardships imply an asset well worth the investment. Thus, a long time before, with Erectus, natural selection worked on ways to promote metabolic efficiency: Long legs for covering territory, an upright stance to free up the hands, sweat glands for endurance, plus the means to store extra body fat to survive times of want.

In addition, the Erectus brain benefited from its own set of metabolic efficiencies: A body with a brain intelligent enough to tame fire and figure out cooking, for instance, was able to digest a far wider range of food in a far shorter time. And—thanks to a certain variation to the gene FOXP2— Erectus possessed enough basic language skills to facilitate their hunting and gathering.

But tell that to Eve, now stuck with the immediate disadvantage of an even bigger brain. Evolution is not a conscious choice. If so, some distant mother down the line would have opted to stick with the same grey matter that served Erectus so well over the previous two million years. Instead, a pair of random copying errors to promoter regions to the genes ARHGAP11BA and HARE5 kept the production line pumping out more neocortical cells than usual.

This would have been a gradual process, over tens of thousands of years, but now we're talking critical mass. Eve's fragile body is supporting what amounts to a massive energy sink, and she is not going to live long enough to cotton on to its hidden advantages. With a bit of luck, she may survive long enough to reproduce and so pass on her genes for one more generation, but she is one food shortage away from her and her entire line coming to a precipitous close. Like everything else in natural selection, we are talking about a series of accidents.

It's not as if an intelligent designer just decided to slap an extra pair of frontal lobes onto Erectus, thereby turning our new Eve prototype into a sapient master of the universe. The reality is that our frontal cortex bears the same proportions relative to the rest of our brain as does the chimp and other primates.

This means that as our cortical areas increased in absolute size, so did our limbic regions. Recall the "triune brain," this evolutionary retrofit of two mammalian layers stacked atop a reptilian brain stem. This arrangement strongly suggests an incomplete and imperfect brain, with

125

competing operating systems—thinking and emotions—in a state of perpetual war, with unpredictable and problematic outcomes.

But if that were truly the case—if living by our emotions were truly that maladaptive—our limbic system should be proportionately smaller by now, vestigial almost. It was one of those knock-me-over-with-a-feather moments when I researched this book and it bears emphasis— proportionately, our brains replicate those of our primate cousins. With a larger cortex, we also inherited a larger limbic system.

Otherwise, by now, we would be on our way to looking like those alien invaders in 1950s movies, with bulging crowns and foreheads. Instead, we are walking around with large and robust limbic systems seamlessly wired into our decidedly unostentatious cortical regions. This integration is so tight that often it's best to think of the amygdala and PFC and their interconnecting regions as one unit.

In a 2006 article in *Discover* magazine, Robert Sapolsky—who pops up everywhere in our discussion of the biology of human behavior—points out that to be human we needn't have evolved unique genes that code for novel types of neurons or neurotransmitters or a more complex frontal cortex and such. Instead, "our braininess as a species arises from having humongous numbers of just a few types of off-the-rack neurons and from the exponentially greater number of interactions between them."

Recall our humble sea snail, with virtually identical neurons to us. We're not special. It's just that we have a lot more of these particular cells (100 billion vs 20,000), which opens the way to an infinity of connections.

A lot of the new brain research is concentrated on mapping these connections, with a view to better understanding how the brain works as a whole. In 2009, the NIMH announced "The Human Connectome Project," a $40 million undertaking with the brief of mapping the 100 trillion ways that our 100 billion neurons hook up.

To give you a mental image, simply picture the internet—the web—with its infinite thread-like strands that self-organize around numerous hubs into a host of overlapping and seamless nonlinear networks. With this kind of map, it is much easier to place our emotions in context, as adding a vital extra dimension to our thinking.

Seen this way, we get a much better handle on understanding our illness. Typically, bipolar is represented as a condition where our emotions tend to get the better of us, and to a large extent this is true. But we always need to keep in mind that without bursts of emotion, our higher cognition would have nothing to work with. Laying down memory, learning, making decisions, motivation, empathy, finding meaning in our lives—all that and more would be virtual nonstarters without our emotions in the mix.

Indeed, we can make a strong case that our thinking is strictly auxiliary to our emotions. The brain science is coming in loud and clear on this—we typically make up our minds before we have a chance to think. As we have already discovered, our subsequent "thinking" simply rationalizes what our emotions—often unconsciously—have already decided.

This explains why we are totally incompetent when it comes to making important decisions, such as voting for a political candidate. We make a horrible mess of it. Too often, we lack the basic intelligence to even vote for our own narrow self-interests.

Paradoxically, once we recognize the limits in our ability to "think," it is much easier to appreciate the enormous adaptive advantage that even a tiny boost in cortical power confers. We are a long way from evolving into pointy-eared Vulcans inerrantly making the perfect rational decision, but as highly resourceful animals, we are the envy of all life forms we haven't yet gotten around to killing off.

Thus, thankfully for us, Eve did live long enough to reproduce.

Alas! Poor Erectus, rest in peace. Everywhere we went, our close human cousins disappeared. Such is the crucial differential between a bigger brain and smaller one. When all is said and done, we are nothing special. We're simply glorified chimps with brains supersized by a pair or more of random copying errors.

Okay, now we need to challenge that notion. Yes, size matters, but let's speculate about a freak accident of genes and nature, one that conferred Eve and her line with a decisive advantage, one that made all the difference, one that in one mighty snap of some cosmic finger delivered us from the brink of extinction to masters of our own destiny.

It's an improbable story, but so is everything else in nature. Let's proceed ...

19

200,000 YEARS AGO: ENVIRONMENT, EPIGENETICS, AND HIGHER INTELLIGENCE

TIMELINE: Still the sixth day of creation, but a bit back when Eve is in the womb. For the purposes of this narrative, we're going to turn our mitochondrial Eve into a real Eve of sorts by giving her a hypothetical evolutionary upgrade, one so significant that it separates her from all who came before her.

A lot is going on in Eve's fetal development. Promoter regions in her DNA are switching on genes that are overseeing the building of cells that will differentiate into organs and systems, including the brain and the nervous system. Eve's developing brain will further differentiate into two separate but connected hemispheres, left and right.

The process is called lateralization and goes way back to before mammals ever walked the earth. Sometime in our distant past, though, our brains became slightly asymmetrical, and the next stage in Eve's fetal development will soon display even more of this.

Could this be the Darwinian game-changer?

Asymmetry evolved as a means for one half of the brain to take on certain tasks in order for the other half to attend to other duties. This allows chickens, for instance, to focus on their food with one eye while watching out for predators with the other.

Similarly, we can make a case that localizing language processing to the left hemisphere enhances overall cognitive performance. Lest we get too carried away with right brain-left brain dichotomies, though, we need to keep in mind that neither hemisphere flies solo. Via a bundle of connecting neural fibers known as the corpus callosum, the two halves remain tightly integrated.

Anyway ...

Back in 2001, at the first psychiatric conference I attended in my new incarnation as a mental health journalist, I happened to run into Amar Klar, head of developmental genetics at the National Cancer Institute. Earlier in his career, Dr Klar had worked on yeast cells at Cold Spring Harbor Laboratory under James Watson of Watson and Crick fame. Dr Klar related to me what appeared to be a crazy idea that had to do with one gene being responsible for both psychosis and left-handedness. I hardly understood a word of it, other than the fact that our primate cousins do not exhibit our decided preference for one hand over the other.

In humans, handedness is pronounced, with nine in 10 of us favoring our right hand. Keep in mind that the left side of the brain governs the right side of the body. So far, so good. But what this had to do with psychosis totally eluded me. Nevertheless, I filed our conversation in the back of my head.

So it was, six years later when I came across an article by Oxford psychiatrist Timothy Crow in the *American Journal of Psychiatry* that also discussed handedness in relation to psychosis, I paid close attention.

It is safe to regard Dr Crow as a founding father of modern schizophrenia research. Back in 1976, using first-generation brain scan technology, he and his colleagues identified ventricular enlargement—ie larger cranial cavities—in the brains of those with schizophrenia. These showed up on each scan as a large black butterfly.

The finding provided early confirmation of the biological basis of schizophrenia. "Bollocks!" someone scrawled across a library copy of the *Lancet*, where the study was published. This apparently represented some form of a Freudian last gasp.

Soon after, Dr Crow was pioneering research into dopamine's role in schizophrenia. Later, he came up with a scheme for classifying positive and negative symptoms in the illness. In the course of his work, he has linked schizophrenia to both language deficits and a disruption in lateralization. Incidentally, four in ten of those with schizophrenia are left-handed.

This, of course, led to Dr Crow digging deeper. Here, mainstream genetics proved a major disappointment. At best, in studies, candidate "psychosis" genes turn up as infinitesimally small statistical blips. These findings raise the suggestion that illnesses such as bipolar and schizophrenia are caused by many genes acting together, each with a small effect.

But would a "big bang" offer a better explanation? Dr Crow believes that our capacity for language evolved relatively abruptly—about 200,000 years ago—and that susceptibility to schizophrenia is the price we pay for this gift. This suggests that both our higher capacity for language and our disposition for schizophrenia may have occurred at the same time.

Perhaps in the same prehistoric womb? Could this be our big bang? If so, how would genetics account for this? The short answer is don't bet on genetics. Enter the science of "epigenetics."

Epigenetics, among other things, accounts for why identical twins are not exactly identical, especially when one twin starts manifesting symptoms of bipolar or schizophrenia while the other remains perfectly healthy. Statistically, if one identical twin shows bipolar symptoms there is roughly a 50-50 chance of the other twin becoming symptomatic, as well. This is a much higher rate than amongst fraternal twins and other family members, not to mention the general public. Simple statistics, then, constitute our best evidence that bipolar is transmitted genetically, even if we cannot identify the genes.

But those same studies also make a compelling case for environmental factors. Why only a 50-50 probability? Why not 70 or 80 or 90 percent? The only explanation is environment. Separate those twins for even a short time—say put them in different classrooms—and they will be growing up with different life experiences. Duplicate seeds, in effect, different soil.

We're right back to Robert Sapolsky's first principles, now, where we're talking about genetic predispositions rather than genetic inevitabilities. It's always a two-step between genes and environment, but now we're introducing a facilitating factor.

Epigenetics literally translates to "above the genes." The field is so new that back in late 2003, when I entered both "epigenetics" and "bipolar" into a PubMed search, I came up with but one scientist conducting actual research. A current search tells a different story, and today epigenetics is emerging as a new frontier in science, one that may eventually provide the answers into the complex dynamics between genes and environment, not to mention yield credible insights into our behavior.

The thinking is that epigenetics acts as a rapid responder to environmental change. This would involve switching genes on or off by means other than those initiated by our regulatory strands of DNA. Thus—

130

and this is well-established—a molecular methyl group may insert itself into a gene portion of DNA and either activate it or silence it. These are fairly routine occurrences, and may account in large part for our reactions to stress, and why, for instance, people exposed to traumatic events may almost overnight develop a sensitized limbic system all too quick to set off fight or flight.

Okay, this is where it gets interesting. Until recently it was believed that what happens inside your life experience stays inside your life experience. That your kids, for instance, wouldn't inherit your trauma. Instead, your DNA could be counted on to build in your offspring a reasonable replica of the same standard-issue amygdala or hippocampus you and your partner were born with, scrubbed free of your pain and suffering.

Epigenetics says not so fast. Our best support for this comes from the "Dutch Hunger Winter" of 1944-45, when the occupying Nazis cut off food supplies to the urban civilian population in the Netherlands. This resulted in some 22,000 deaths. Thanks to meticulous records kept by the Dutch, we know that those exposed to the starvation conditions as early term fetuses turned out as adults to have higher rates of obesity and greater susceptibility to a range of illnesses (including schizophrenia).

This of itself shouldn't be too surprising. We already know that the body will store fat in starvation conditions, and that failure to reset to normal during subsequent times of plenty will likely result in obesity. It also should come as no surprise that those exposed to starvation in utero will contend with these same challenges. The big surprise, though, is that their kids—the offspring of those who survived the hunger winter inside the womb—in turn are experiencing higher rates of obesity and bad health. How can this be?

Our prime suspect is insulin-like growth factor 2 (IGF2), a gene that looms large in growth during gestation. Recent research reveals that those who had experienced the famine during that crucial early stage in their fetal development showed less DNA methylation in this gene compared to their siblings.

Let this sink in for a second: What the Dutch Winter Hunger is telling us is that an extremely stressful event your grandmother may have experienced in the womb may have a profound impact on your physical or mental state in the here and now. Or, to freely extrapolate, a trauma that may have affected your great-granddad as a boy may still be echoing in your brain a century later.

Boggles the mind, doesn't it? Meanwhile, 200,000 years ago ...

131

So here we have our hypothetical Eve, a barely differentiated embryo inside her mother's uterus. What is going on outside? The Pleistocene equivalent of a hunger winter? If that is the case—we're wildly speculating, here—Eve's lack of nutrition is setting off epigenetic alarm bells. The logical response would be some kind of metabolic quick fix. A restructuring to Eve's most metabolically demanding organ, perhaps. Her brain is still under construction. Maybe we can deviate from the standard genetic blueprint. Maybe we can move some neurons around, while we still have a chance.

Are there any available genes that can be recruited to accomplish this? A convenient target for a methyl group to attach to? Dr Crow has his eye on Protocadherin 11X/Y, that facilitates cell adhesion.

To bring this back to earth: It is important to note that Dr Crow's work is blazing new research trails into how our brains work (or fail to work) in the here and now. The more we learn about lateralization, the more we will learn about psychosis and how to treat it and possibly prevent it. Digging out an evolutionary history, even a speculative one, will deepen our understanding.

So—going with our wild speculation scenario—we have an epigenetically enhanced Eve emerging into the world, with a metabolically more efficient brain, one that just happens to confer an unprecedented new language skillset—an accident, the latest in a series of accidents.

As it turned out, Eve survived long enough to pass on this skillset to the next generation. In a small and isolated population, evolutionary change can be explosive, especially with a host of extreme environmental pressures weeding out the maladaptors.

Language is the gateway to higher reasoning and more complex social organization. Next thing—well, give it about 150,000 years—we have our new Masters of the Pleistocene venturing out of Africa and rubbing elbows with the Neanderthal (not for the first time). Here, in lieu of any surviving eye-witness accounts, we can frame the narrative anyway we wish: The geeks outsmart the jocks, the cool kids snub the dorks. Just to make it interesting, a little bit of hanky-panky goes on, with some of their DNA landing in our genome.

Funny thing about the Neanderthal. Their brains were even larger than ours. Taking into account their more robust bodies and other factors, though, scientists estimate that their grey matter scales roughly the same. So here we have a mysterious population of Homo, so genetically similar to us that some experts regard them as fellow Sapiens. Most likely, they branched off from Erectus somewhere outside of Africa and found their way to Europe, where they developed a suite of gene variations built for survival in Ice Age conditions. It was our good luck that enough of these particular gene variations just happened to land in our DNA.

The archaeological record the Neanderthal left is remarkably similar to Eve's Erectus descendants, with the same types of tools and artwork and so on, that is until about 70,000 years ago. While the Neanderthal were content to turn out the same work they always had, Sapiens experienced a sort of technological and cultural Renaissance.

In his 2015 best-seller, *Sapiens: A Short History*, Israeli historian Yuval Hariri attributes this "cognitive revolution" to a mysterious evolutionary upgrade. Overnight, it seems, with Brain 2.0, we were splashing paint on cave walls and hunting big game to extinction. Could it be that relocating language to the left hemisphere came 130,000 years later than Dr Crow's estimates? Or did it take Eve's descendants all that time to fully figure out the operating system?

Perhaps it was enough that Eve and her immediate descendants had more metabolically efficient brains to get them through inevitable food shortages. Her later descendants could unlock the system's new killer language apps all in good time.

Or perhaps Eve was able to able to find some kind of immediate selective advantage. Maybe, she used her new operating system to extract small favors from the others in her band. Maybe she used it to help her band exploit a new food source. In either case, we're implying a higher level of cooperation—including manipulation—than went on before. The type of advantage that would get her through a harsh winter and into the mating game come spring.

With no prehistoric brains to study, we will never know what went on. What we do know, though is that very soon after, relatively speaking, Eve's descendants would be the only humans left standing. Thanks to our unique brain power, we became walking mass extinction machines on the cusp of building great civilizations.

From climbing out of trees to sitting in office buildings—that's our story and we're sticking to it.

But our genes—including any methyl groups clinging to them—have a different tale to tell. If we go with our wildly speculative scenario, their solution to the extreme environmental challenge that Eve faced inside the womb was not language and higher cognition. No, from their vantage point, in response to a Code Red metabolic emergency, our genetic masters were merely moving around neurons, from the right side of one unfinished brain to the other.

With at most a few thousand Sapiens on the planet, extinction would have been the outcome of failure. It didn't turn out that way. A problem solved for our collection of replicators. An unexpected boon for the vehicle.

20

TWELVE THOUSAND YEARS AGO: SOMETHING IS ABOUT TO GO SERIOUSLY WRONG

TIMELINE: The sixth day of creation—again. We are out of Africa and into the lands of the Bible.

We now find ourselves in the middle of a modern mystery: The brains of Eve's descendants have unaccountably grown smaller. Not just slightly smaller, a full ten percent smaller, as in what you might reasonably gouge out of the contents of a skull with a small ice cream scoop.

The reduction coincides with the introduction of agriculture some 10 to 12 thousand years ago. One entirely reasonable explanation is that perhaps our already highly integrated neural connections became even more integrated, which resulted in our brains making fewer metabolic demands. Form followed function. Soon—diminished but enhanced—we were setting the stage for our great leap forward into civilization.

A contrasting explanation has us acknowledging the introduction of agriculture for the initial disaster it had to have been. Overnight, we went from a rich and varied hunter-gatherer diet to dependence on one or two varieties of grain. Making a bad situation worse, settling into one place only encouraged reproduction and its attendant population pressures, including exposure to all manner of diseases. Thus, severely malnourished, we found ourselves once again facing a major metabolic crisis. In response, our bodies scaled down (by some five inches in males), and our brains, with their disproportionate metabolic demands, even more so.

135

A modern example of this occurring is the two-or-three inch height disparity between the North and South Koreans—the former exposed to famine during the nineties—both who share the same ancestral genes.

We can also make a case that as we shifted from hunter-gatherers living off our wits to agriculturalists performing routine tasks, Mother Nature—that cold and ruthless bookkeeper—invariably chose to downsize.

Even brains are expendable. The sea squirt, for instance, spends the first part of its life swimming around in the ocean. Once it lodges securely to a rock and settles in, it eats its brain for energy. It's true—sometimes thinking is highly overrated. And often we think entirely too much for our own good.

Kurt Vonnegut built a whole novel around this idea. In his 1985 *Galapagos*, a small group of island castaways are the only survivors of a worldwide pandemic. As generations pass, survival and reproduction favor those who can dive for fish. Those with smaller brains and more streamlined skulls have the decided advantage. By the end of the book, their descendants morphologically resemble seals, but who have nonetheless retained that vital trait that makes them uniquely human—the ability to laugh at farts.

Keep in mind, it is more instructive for us to think of ourselves as highly resourceful animals rather than "thinking" beings. Rational thought is a Platonic ideal that we are a long way from achieving. We're not wired to "think" with any convincing degree of reliability. In this regard, "Sapien" is a total misnomer.

We were wired, though, to outwit the competition, form social alliances, and respond creatively to novel situations. For instance, that dinner invitation from a stranger—does that involve you being the guest of honor or the main course? That person close to you who tells you not to worry, should you be intensely worried?

Emotions give us some pretty good indicators, but "thinking" provides the vital nuances. Typically, we fail to appreciate our frontal regions until they happen to go off-line. Whether we're talking about depression or mania, anxiety, ADD, or psychosis—whether we find ourselves shutting down or amping up, whether immobilized or running wild, frozen in fear or recklessly fearless—inevitably, when things go wrong, it comes down to the front end of the brain having lost its capacity to work with the back end of the brain.

It bears repeating that our neural circuitry is so seamlessly integrated that when it comes to processing certain specific tasks, it is best to regard different sections of the brain as one unit, if only fleetingly. It's hardly a perfect setup, but when everything is working optimally we are wonders to behold. We live off our wits—that tightly choreographed series of exchanges between our instant reactions and more considered responses. Seen in this light, a towering intellect is strictly optional. Perhaps, then, it is best to think of ourselves as Homo Resourceful, not Sapien.

Maybe we can academicize it to Homo Resourcefulianus. So ...

Going back to our wildly speculative scenario involving our latest upgrade to our operating system—the one having to do with the consolidation of our language capabilities to the left hemisphere—overnight we had the symbols to think abstractly and communicate socially, with the enhanced ability to learn from past experience as well as to plan ahead. At the same time, we lived in the type of challenging environment that would have nurtured the development of these new skills.

Importantly, our emotions would have provided strong cues. Imagine, for instance, the rush of dopamine from the thrill of knapping the next-generation spear point. Imagine that same rush over that spear point bringing down an antelope, a class of animal that most likely eluded our Erectus cousins. Imagine, also, the high degree of planning and social organization that went into the hunt, all facilitated by our new communications skills. Savor the taste of the cooked meat. Savor the dopamine. Life is good.

Perhaps, then, we need to think of thought as serving emotions, not the other way around. True, emotion may give meaning to thought, but the opposite may apply with much greater force—thought gives meaning to emotions. It's all very well that our ability to solve intellectual puzzles gives us a decisive selective advantage. But when all is said and done, our purpose in life is far less exalted. Simply put, we are here to rise to whatever occasion nature may happen to dump on us. Then bask in the reward.

Thus far, our resourceful brains have proved worthy of the challenge. But take away those challenges and opportunities and see what happens. We're back to rats and mice again. Take a rodent and stick it in a deprived environment, with no social or other stimulation, and watch it shut down. Recall that these are your creatures that will choose sipping the drug-laced water every time.

The same rats in enriched environments, you will remember, tend to ignore the drug-water. They have better things to do.

You can argue all you want about life in the Pleistocene being nasty, brutish, and short. But you would be hard-pressed to make a convincing case that it did not confer more than its share of satisfying, dopamine-inducing, challenges. But that would soon change. We have just been served our eviction notice from the Garden. Evolution is about to take a wrong turn at agriculture.

21

SIX THOUSAND YEARS AGO: DOMESTICATING THE HUMAN HERD

THE SIXTH day of creation—again. The Book of Genesis mentions a river flowing out of Eden that separated into four headwaters. These include two that became identified with the Cradle of Civilization.

Sometime around eight thousand years ago, a group of neolithic farmers came down from the hills with their dogs and goats and settled on the flood plains bordered by the Tigris and Euphrates, in the land of Sumer, what is today southern Iraq.

Like their counterparts elsewhere, these farmers were skilled in taming the land, building dwellings and other structures, and in fashioning a new generation of tools and clothing and possessions. This implied a higher level of cooperation and social organization than back when we were hunter-gatherers, but the settled life also introduced a new breed of human into the ecosystem—the opportunist, humans who preyed on fellow humans.

No doubt, this breed existed in our hunter-gatherer days, as well, but with no accumulated wealth to acquire or special privileges to gain, the benefits would have been minimal—a scrap of food here, a fleeting mating opportunity there. Weighed against the risks—such as a spear point being righteously shoved into one's skull—the best survival option would have been a strategy of brotherly and sisterly love, kumbaya and all that.

But that all changed once there was wealth to be had, a system to be gamed. In nothing flat, the playing field tipped in favor of the opportunist. A lot of academic debate, especially in the form of game theory, has centered on the comparative advantages of opportunism and aggression vs cooperation and altruism. The conversation is highly esoteric and nuanced, but a consensus seems to have emerged that although it is in the best interests of the group for its members to cooperate, there will always be those who find it to their individual advantage to cheat.

There is also consensus that the best way of policing the cheaters involves "tit for tat." "I will trust you not to mess with me until you mess with me," is how our society rolls. This is supported by numerous computer models. These same models also show that things fall apart when everyone trusts everyone or no one trusts anyone.

We may live in a highly competitive dog-eat-dog world, but we operate within tightly integrated social structures based on conditional trust and cooperation. Families and cities and corporations and nation states could not function, otherwise. But ...

What if it's a lie? What if coercion is really the glue that is holding our society together? What if a lot of what we call trust and cooperation is simply nothing more than blind obedience? And what if we're too dumb to see through the illusion?

We're back to our modern mystery—involving our unaccountably smaller brains—with our band of trusting and naive agriculturalists venturing into a new land, about to unwittingly build their own Orwellian Animal Farm. As in previous chapters, we're in the realm of wild speculation, but let's run with it ...

What went down was the construction of the world's first massive public works project, one that required a separation of land from water in the form of dams and channels, both for irrigation and drainage. We're deep into the Book of Genesis now, during the time of the Great Flood.

Each spring, the waters of the Tigris and Euphrates gushed across a vast plain that received no rainfall, leaving behind a thick layer of nutrient-rich muck. The floods clearly made settlement problematic, but nonetheless offered possibilities. So it was that a new labor force picked up their tools and dug in. But someone or some group had to have been calling the shots. Someone had to have been giving orders, with the power to enforce them.

If you happen to believe that those toiling in the hot sun, waste deep in the muck, were imagining a better future for themselves and their children, perhaps you can convince yourself that everyone pitched in willingly, in the interests of the greater good.

But how long would that have lasted? How long till some started protesting their lot and others began ruing the day they were born? How long till the cheaters in the crowd came up with ways to reap the benefits of everyone else's sweat and toil? How long till the first lash drew blood?

If only someone had been taking notes.

Years pass, centuries, a millennia. We now have the successful integration of two different rivers into an intricate latticework of waterways and arable land. An unexpected byproduct of this effort is a quantum leap into civilization, and we have the archaeological remains to prove it—networked cities on a scale never before imagined, supported by agricultural abundance.

"Walk on the wall of Uruk," an ancient author boasts. "Follow its course around the city, inspect its mighty foundations, examine its brickwork, how masterfully it is built!"

The ancient author is chronicling the glory of the mythic king, Gilgamesh. But there is a note of discord. We read of an arrogant king, his head raised high, "trampling its citizens like a wild bull."

Clearly there is trouble in paradise. But not to worry. This is the natural order, we are informed in so many words in another ancient text. Work is difficult, but—hey!—someone has to plow and harvest and build walls and maintain those silted up irrigation channels and all the rest. And that is why the Gods created man, we are told, so the Gods wouldn't have to do the work, themselves.

When man complained, the Gods sent down a plague, followed by a flood.

So maybe someone was taking meticulous notes, after all.

If you look at this from the perspective of a Sumerian god (or the lucky few entrusted with ruling on their behalf), a few plagues and a flood are a very efficient way of culling your human livestock, especially if you aim your microbes and thunderbolts (or bronze spear points) at the smart people and rabble-rousers. Within just a few generations, your breeding program will produce precisely the type of dumb and compliant humans you need to do your heavy lifting for you.

This, after all, is how we domesticate animals.

"Natural slaves," was the term Aristotle would use centuries later. "Indeed," he wrote with apparent approval, "the use made of slaves and of tame animals is not very different."

141

Have a look at your watch. If it's an analogue display, you are looking at a Sumerian inspiration. To them goes the credit for dividing the circle into 360 degrees and the day into minutes and hours.

But next time you find yourself checking the time, ask yourself the reason. Chances are you are laboring under a deadline for work that you find totally unrewarding for the benefit of someone you may resent absolutely. This, too, is the Sumerian legacy.

We're veering a bit off the evolutionary psychology script now. The basic story line there is that our environment changed entirely too fast over the last 10,000 years for evolution to have caught up. Essentially, our modern skulls house a Stone Age mind. Lacking the full Darwinian toolkit to adapt to today's challenges, it's no surprise that we get depressed and anxious and turn to alcohol and drugs and so on.

Evolutionary psychology also provides credible explanations for why the full panoply of our modern behavior—from feeling threatened to forming social alliances to finding a mate—makes perfect sense in a world tens and hundreds of thousands of years removed from our own.

Anxiety, for instance, was a basic Stone Age survival tool. Those who exhibited more laid-back tendencies sooner or later ended up in some cave bear's belly. Depression, in the meantime, was a way of realistically viewing your options and taking stock.

Even bipolar comes across as almost normal when you consider that, like all life forms, we cycle in accord with the seasons. Winter depressions equated to hibernation, when we needed to shut down and conserve energy. Mania, by contrast, tends to be a warm weather phenomenon, a time for adventure, reproductive and otherwise.

But then we have to start asking ourselves harder questions, and here the answers point to the disturbing likelihood of ancient eugenics projects along the river systems of the ancient world.

In this dystopian context, we were born to be wild, but we were bred to be compliant. Those who resisted did not live long enough to pass on their genes. In all likelihood, we created a new species of human, one well-adapted to follow orders and perform the simple tasks demanded by the new world order. Strictly speaking, then, we are not exactly Stone Age minds housed in modern skulls. Far from it, actually, having regard for the fact that Eve's massive brain wouldn't even fit inside our puny little heads. Send us back in time to her world and we wouldn't last five minutes.

From Homo Resourcefulianus to Homo Compliantus. Could it be that evolution took one giant leap backward? It could be that civilization was one huge mistake?

142

22

THE FOURTH CENTURY BCE: THE RULE OF THE SOCIOPATH

TIMELINE: In the shadow of the Book of Genesis, several thousand years into what I would describe as the Common Narrative, one that traces the ascent of humankind from the first cities along the Tigris and Euphrates to the almost unbroken march of progress into the present.

But are the purveyors of the Common Narrative telling us the truth?

We pick up the story sometime in the twelfth century BCE, with the flourishing Mycenaean culture of mainland Greece and its surrounding islands and outposts—the center of a vast trading network that extended from the Black Sea to the Nile and further afield.

The catch was that the new benefits generated by trade only accrued to a small ruling class and the elites serving them. Basically, the Mediterranean way of life aped ancient Sumerian custom.

Then, literally overnight, civilization mysteriously collapsed, and this part of the world entered into an extended dark ages. Contemporary accounts refer to an enigmatic "Sea People" who seemed to have swooped out of nowhere, destroying everything in their path.

Hundreds of years later, civilization rebooted, but with a somewhat reshuffled social deck. A new class of producers and merchants and artisans asserted themselves. This opened the way for a novel breed of deep-thinkers who would change everything.

Classical Greece's time in the sun was short, but over the next two and a half millennia, its achievements inspired every leap forward in what we would later call western civilization—from eye-popping and mind-blowing art and architecture and philosophy and literature to passing the cultural torch to the Romans to infusing new life into Judaism to laying the theological bedrock to Christianity to providing the intellectual backbone to the Islamic high culture of the Middle Ages to kickstarting the Renaissance to inspiring the scientific and philosophical revolutions of the sixteen and seventeen hundreds to the founding of the United States.

Even today, these ancient Greeks turn up everywhere in our school curricula.

So far, so good. But our Golden Age is no sooner up and running than an assembly of righteous Athenians puts Socrates on a hemlock diet. This leads his student, Plato, to deeply distrust the dictates of the mob, who are too ignorant to think and decide in anyone's best interests, much less their own. Plato, instead, placed his stock in the idea of an enlightened philosopher-king. His own student, Aristotle, actually set about educating one.

Enter Alexander the Great, Aristotle's most famous student—opportunist, narcissist, sociopath.

Let's begin with Mr Great's family background. His mother was the fiery and cunning Olympias of Epirus, his father Zeus, king of the gods. The matter of paternity, incidentally, came straight from the mouth of the great one, himself, and was attested to by none other than his mother, who was presumably there at the time in question.

There is no disputing Alexander's vision, intellect, military genius, charisma, physical courage, and leadership skills. Men willingly followed him into battle over the course of ten years (even more, counting when his human father, Philip, ran the show), enduring every imaginable privation along the way. It is 324 BCE. Following an exhausting Indian campaign and a death march through a baking desert, he and the remnants of his army are back inside Persia, nowhere near close to returning to Greece or nearby Macedonia.

Alexander has trained his sights on Arabia. The Macedonian contingent of his army is having second thoughts. They are ready to mutiny, as they had two years before in India. It's time for our fearless leader to give the standard Shakespearean "Band of Brothers" speech. And he sort of does this by reminding them how his other father of convenience—Philip of Macedonia, not Zeus—turned them from hide-clad vagabond shepherds into proud men and rulers.

A note about this other father of his. Philip once tried to kill him in a drunken brawl. Fortunately, Olympias, in a display of maternal concern, conveniently paid her retainers to have her human husband whacked. Alexander may have had two putative fathers, but we are detecting signs of an over-indulged mother's boy.

If we're looking for emotional attachments, by the way, Alexander most likely shared his deepest bond with his horse, Bucephalus. When his trusty mount died in India, our grief-stricken hero named a city after him. Too bad he lacked the same regard for his men. Back to his speech ...

Instead of building on his Band of Brothers theme, our son of Zeus unaccountably makes the discourse all about himself. It was he and his cavalry, he reminds his men, who conquered Persia. No mention of his long-suffering spear-carriers. Those lucky enough to have tagged along with him, he lets them know, he granted the spoils of war and bestowed great honors. As for those who died in battle, didn't they all receive splendid burials?

Really, I'm not making this up.

"Depart!" he commands. "Go back and report at home that your king Alexander, the conqueror of the Persians, Medes, Bactrians, and Sacians ..." The list goes on and on. And on.

And it would have been a much larger list, he lets them know in mid-list, had they not lost their nerve in India and compelled him to turn back. Nevertheless, he has graciously led them back into Persia through the waterless Desert of Gedrosia, "where no one ever before marched with an army."

About Gedrosia—present-day southern Balochistan above the Arabian Sea—where temperatures of 120 F are routine: Twelve thousand men failed to complete the 60-day journey, with no splendid funerals in consolation. In all likelihood, Gedrosia was an enraged Alexander's way of punishing his men for not indulging him in his whim of conquering India.

Now to close the deal: "Report that when you returned to Susa you deserted him [ie Alexander] and went away, handing him over to the protection of conquered foreigners."

A classic example of gaslighting, a good two and a bit millennia prior to the invention of the gaslight.

A final sarcastic flourish, then, once again: "Depart!"

History records that Alexander immediately leapt down from the platform he was standing on and retired to his quarters, leaving his dumbstruck men unable to decide what to do next. Three or four days later, they could take it no more. Approaching his tent, they threw down their weapons and prostrated themselves before him, begging forgiveness.

So why did Alexander's men put up with all this? And how did Alexander get away with it, in the first place? In her 2007 book, *Evil Genes*, Barbara Oakley, citing numerous sources, refers to the Alexanders of the world as the "successfully sinister" or "high-machs" (for Machiavellian)—highly manipulative sociopaths with strong elements of borderline personality disorder and narcissism, not to mention paranoia, who specialize in leaving a long trail of broken lives in their paths.

Dr Oakley's model "borderpath" was Chairman Mao, who was responsible for more deaths under his watch as China's "Great Helmsman" than the likes of Hitler and Stalin combined. His long-time personal physician described him as "devoid of human feeling, incapable of love, friendship, or warmth." Classic sociopathic traits, but we also see borderline tendencies that included a certain lack of continuity with his own identity. In all probability, Mao did not even believe in Communism. As he said of himself: "My words and my deeds are inconsistent."

Dr Oakley also pays regard to delusional thinking, a trait common amongst conspiracy theorists, as well. These are people who are capable of maintaining their crackpot beliefs with great conviction in complete defiance of the facts. Our best illustration here is Hitler, who could always rationalize as legitimate his every action, no matter how bizarre and contrary to human nature.

Once again, we are left scratching our heads. "How did they do it?" we wonder. "How did they get away with it?"

We tend to identify sociopaths as the type of people who fill up our prisons. But the smart and privileged ones capable of controlling their impulses and putting their manipulative skills to the fore are typically found occupying top positions in business and politics and academia. Although they comprise a very small minority of the population—one or two percent—by virtue of their top dog status, their influence is enormous. These are the people who poison our culture and who set the tone for the toxic environments we are forced to contend with, whether in the workplace or the public sphere.

In our daily lives, we encounter their less exalted versions—the abusive boss, the back-stabbing colleague, the unfeeling partner, and the family member who drives everyone nuts. If we're lucky, they only ruin our days. Too often, they ruin our lives.

The rest of us are no match for this breed. If this were a game of chess, the successfully sinister are typically four moves ahead. Recall that thanks to ancient eugenics programs, the playing field has long ago been tilted in their favor. They literally feed off the naive and over-compliant. Moreover —unkindest cut of all—they excel in recruiting their victims to do their bidding for them.

It's crazy, but the status quo seems to operate on our apparent willingness to give up on the one life we have in order to please the very people who least deserve to breathe the same air we do. Whether it's some hapless hoplite in Alexander's army we are talking about or an unappreciated "human resource" in a corporation, we not only find ourselves powerless to put up a fight, but we seem incapable of even imagining a better life for ourselves.

Put a lab rat through the experimental hoops—hang it by the tail, force it to swim—and they will quickly reach a state of immobilization and learned helplessness. These rats, incidentally, respond well to antidepressants, perhaps better than we do. This strongly suggests that our equivalent mental states run far deeper and exact way more of a personal toll than is good for us. Thanks to our perversely more advanced brains, we are capable of thinking our way into the type of life-sucking black holes that no antidepressant can penetrate and relieve.

Tragically, our adaptive response tends to favor psychically anesthetizing ourselves—becoming emotionally numb—cutting ourselves off from our thoughts and feelings, from our true sense of self. Call it depression, if you want, but it's far more than that. In our state of extreme personal alienation—of nowhere men and women living in our nowhere land—we find it only natural to cede our own personal sovereignty to those who deserve it least.

Walk into any depression or bipolar support group and you will get a feel for the human toll. Far too many stories involve broken lives from workplace abuse. Once the inevitable trauma and depression set in, along with the learned helplessness and all the rest, return to the life one had before becomes highly problematic. Many, if not most, of these people have strong and admirable qualities. But even the strongest and most admirable have their breaking points.

If we stick to the Common Narrative, though, we are left with no choice but to accept the fact that that we are losers with broken brains who somehow lost our place in line when all of life's perks were handed out.

Is that what you truly believe?

The Common Narrative serves up a convenient story for moving history forward, in one spectacular burst of human achievement after another, and into a seemingly inevitable present. So inevitable, in fact, that it is virtually impossible to imagine an alternative. Heaven help if we do—society is quick to dismiss original thinkers as dreamers and crackpots. Deep inside, though, we know something is missing. Deep inside, something doesn't feel right. Deep inside, we know that if we accept someone else's story as the definitive one, one that applies to us all, we will never find our way home.

As for Alexander, fortunately this particular story has a happy ending. Soon after verbally abusing his men in his mockery of the standard Band of Brothers speech, our sociopath-narcissist-extraordinaire died in Babylon of mysterious causes. In all likelihood, some of his men finally got smart and poisoned his wine. At long last, they got to go home.

23

THE PRESENT: INTRODUCING HUMANKIND'S ONLY HOMO SAPIEN, EVER

TIMELINE: Day of Judgment. We're into the last Book of the Bible, now, the perfect bookend to the first. From the beginning of Creation, we fast forward to its inevitable destruction and its climactic Apocalypse. Nevertheless, Revelation still holds out hope for a new Heaven on earth. But, to freely interpret, it's going to take a lot more than mere faith in God to make that happen.

We're going to need some very smart people to save the day, ones with first-class brains capable of coming up with alternatives to Armageddon. You know the drill: Find inventive ways of feeding the nine billion people who will soon be over-crowding this planet, reverse global warming, and—most important—reach an international protocol on capping noxious Kenny G emissions. Recently, scientists have concluded that we have unofficially entered a new geological era and they've even given it a name—the Anthropocine—to indicate man's new status as the prime mover in shaping the planet and its ecosystems.

So far, we have proved more than proficient in employing our super powers to beat a path to Armageddon. But are we capable of making a course correction to New Jerusalem? That's one hell of a tall order, no job for intellectual wimps.

149

Our model for the brainy human is John von Neumann, the man who ushered in the age of computers. The story begins more than 70 years ago, with the development of the ENIAC computer and its successor, EDVAC.

These were the work of John Mauchley and J Presper Eckhert for use by the Army's Ballistic Research Laboratory in Aberdeen, Maryland. ENIAC, which came online in 1946, had nearly 18,000 vacuum tubes, weighed 27 tons, and covered 1,800 square feet of floor space. Yet, for all its heft, it was basically a glorified calculating machine.

Then, two years later, came a von Neumann-inspired retrofit that transformed this ungainly beast into essentially the same unit as the device in your hand or what is sitting on your desk. The world would never be the same.

As a boy in Hungary, von Neumann dazzled the adults with his math and memory prowess. Later in life, he would continue to amaze. A colleague put to him a variant of the two-trains-leaving-the-station problem that was the bane of all our lives in high school algebra classes. This one involved a fly streaking back and forth between two bicycles coming from different directions. Von Neumann solved the puzzle instantly.

"I have sometimes wondered whether a brain like von Neumann's does not indicate a species superior to that of man", proclaimed Nobel Laureate Hans Bethe. Edward Teller, father of the H-bomb, remarked that von Neumann could effortlessly carry on a conversation with his three-year-old, as equals, then wondered "if he used the same principle when he talked to the rest of us."

More startling still, von Neumann was not some kind of social oddball. No schizotypal qualities like Einstein, no OCD like Tesla, no breaks with reality like John Nash. He effortlessly socialized, was immensely popular, and enjoyed a happy marriage.

To develop our thesis further, we can advance the argument that von Neumann's braininess was so freakish that he may have constituted humankind's first and only true Homo Sapien.

To please his father, our bright young man studied chemistry in Berlin and then Zurich, but he simultaneously pursued a PhD in math at Budapest. Just to show you how smart he was, within years of graduation he founded the field of game theory, plus came up with the foundational math to quantum physics.

Had they awarded the Fields Medal (for mathematics) back in then, he certainly would have been honored. But by the time they came out with the distinction, von Neumann had passed the age limit. The Fields is a young person's medal.

Ironically, the Nobel, which he was worthy of receiving more than once, is an old person's prize. The distinction tends to go to the near-dead for work performed decades before. Von Neumann, unfortunately, died way too young, before he had a chance to reach esteemed elder status. There are no posthumous honors.

In 1933, still a young man, he came to the US as part of the founding faculty of the Institute of Advanced Study in Princeton, which included Albert Einstein. When World War II broke out, he was recruited for the Manhattan Project. One of his contributions involved figuring out how to detonate the fat boy bomb used on Nagasaki. He was there at Alamogordo for the historic Trinity test.

While working on the A-bomb, he became aware of another top secret project—ENIAC. This wasn't the first computer. The British already had their Colossus up and running—in secret, of course—to crack Nazi codes. More historically significant was that ENIAC was the first computer that came to von Neumann's attention.

Keep in mind, we are talking about a man so ridiculously sapient that he seemed to have a modern computer for a brain. It wasn't just about processing speed or memory. It was flexibility. It was as if every time he turned his mind to something new, all he had to do was install new software to tell the rest of his grey matter what to do. ENIAC originally didn't have this capacity.

In a sense, von Neumann was the only man on the planet with the capability to visualize a new computer to think the way he did. By this time, the developers of ENIAC were already planning EDVAC. It's no surprise that when he joined their conversation, he knew as much about computers as anyone else in the room.

Actually, you could even argue he had a bit of a head start. Back in the 1930s, he had befriended the British mathematician Alan Turing, who would crack the Nazi's Enigma Code with his electro-mechanical device, the Bombe. As part of their idle chit-chat, the two would speculate about artificial intelligence.

Von Neumann's contribution to EDVAC was to suggest configuring the machine in such a way that made software—what they then called programming—the boss. The software told the rest of the computer what to do. When you wanted the computer to perform an entirely different task, instead of taking the machine off-line and spending days moving cables and vacuum tubes around, you simply loaded new software.

Side note: The first generation of programers were women.

ENIAC went online in 1946. In 1948, it received a retrofit that incorporated von Neumann's suggestions. EDVAC debuted in 1949. Von Neumann's own computer at the Institute of Advanced Studies became partly operational in 1951. In 1952, IBM introduced its own commercial mainframe. These and other computers were known initially as von Neumann machines.

This is hardly the end of the story. Von Neumann was also intensely interested in the human brain. Had he lived longer, on top of all his other achievements, it is only fair to assume he would have risen to the top of the field in neuroscience. We can make a case that in the brief time he devoted to the field he did.

In his early fifties, stricken with cancer, he jotted notes for a lecture he had been invited to deliver at Yale University. The title was *Computers and the Brain*. He died before he could complete the task. Nevertheless, in 1958, Yale University published his incomplete notes as a book. The volume, all of 90 pages, mostly white space, is still in print. The most recent edition contains a forward by futurist Ray Kurzweill, head of development at Google and author of the 2005 best-seller, *The Singularity is Near*.

Von Neumann was writing at a time when the brain was still a mysterious black box. Neurotransmitters were virtually unknown, and the frontal lobotomy was still in use as a medical procedure. In this regard, one would expect a laughably naive and absurd commentary. But this is von Neumann we're talking about, not any old genius.

Von Neumann viewed the brain as a processing unit, much like the computer, but with some key differences, the major one involving parallel vs serial processing. The brain is undeniably parallel (as opposed to the computer's serial), with even simple tasks proceeding along numerous pathways before things join up at some stage. Von Neumann compares the brain's neurons to the vacuum tubes that inhabited his computers, but he takes a huge leap into the future by stressing the importance of connectivity.

Recall that connectivity is now all the rage in brain science. It only took about 60 years for our best minds in the field to catch up.

According to von Neumann, vacuum tubes and neurons perform similar tasks, namely receiving, initiating, and transmitting impulses. The pulse going out is shaped by the pulse coming in. In the computer, incoming and outgoing pulses exist in a sort of one-to-one (serial) relationship. The neuron, however, is capable of receiving impulses from numerous other neurons. The single pulse it may send is the result of interpreting all these other pulses.

Understandably, the neuron is going to process information many degrees of magnitude slower than even the most primitive vacuum tube, but it makes up for this deficit through the sheer complexity of its (parallel) connections. In turn, according to von Neumann, all these connecting links (synapses) create a sort of multiplier effect.

If you're thinking that it would be cool to have a computer that combines the processing speed of the most advanced chip sets with the complexity of the human brain, that is probably what von Neumann was thinking, as well, and that day is certainly not too far away. Unfortunately, *Computers and the Brain* ends abruptly, before he could synthesize these thoughts.

More germane to our discussion is the likelihood of repurposing this approach to retooling our own brains. Deep-thinkers such as Ray Kurzweill have been arguing this for years. At a conference in 2014, I heard him make the case for a brain implant that would connect us to a cloud-based super-brain. At the same conference, in reply to a question concerning whether it is possible to create a super-human, geneticist and sequencer of the human genome, Craig Venter, remarked: "If you can define one, we can create one."

When that day comes, say goodbye to Homo Sapiens as a species. Or perhaps, say hello. Recall that the term better refers to a Platonic ideal than to reality. So, perhaps with the aid of technology, we can turn the Homo Resourcefulianus and Homo Compliantus amongst us into our first true generation of Homo Sapiens. The sort of beings we always imagined ourselves to be, but never lived up to. Perhaps tomorrow will herald a new breed of Nietzchean supermen and women, modeled on John von Neumann, ready to save the world.

Or perhaps we will produce a breed of Frankenstein monsters and hasten the arrival of our own Armageddon. Who knows?

Recall that our existence is the result of a series of accidents. The first in the series went back four billion years ago to molecules that began to replicate new versions of themselves.

Five hundred million years ago, in the wake of the Cambrian Explosion, life reached new levels of complexity. One of these had to do with the evolution of primitive neural systems capable of simple learning.

Another accident, this time in the form of a comet that wiped out the dinosaur 65 million years ago, opened the way for mammals and their sophisticated triune brains. The dynamic between the limbic and cortical regions in these new brains laid down the template for much that governs our behavior today.

Fast forward to three million or so years ago where our larger primate brains introduced a new wrinkle into our behavior, namely that we get stressed by each other.

We move a little bit ahead to 200 thousand years ago, with our much larger brains, but bearing the same proportions to our primate cousins. One outcome is a technological and cultural revolution that takes us to the top of the food chain.

We hit our most recent series of accidents 10,000 years ago with the introduction of agriculture and our subsequent crowding into cities. The Common Narrative cites this development as one small step for evolution, one giant leap for civilization. In this book, though we are contending that evolution took a wrong turn at agriculture.

Thanks to the culling of the human herd, we set up the rule of the sociopath, with their naive and compliant subjects brow-beaten into a state of learned helplessness. And all along the way, we were fed the myth that we are sapient beings, worthy of the distinction of Homo Sapien. Now, ironically, having developed the means to take control of our own evolution, we may yet produce precisely this sort of being.

Or not.

It is only by going with this alternative history that we can even begin to come to terms with our felt sense of disconnect, of not belonging. Why is it that we feel so out of place? Why, for so many of us, is adaptation so goddamned hard?

We may delude ourselves that we have a sense of control, but in the final analysis—whether in our own individual lives or contemplating our fate as a species—we know deep down that we are little more than a series of accidents, including accidents waiting to happen. It's a sobering thought, but once we come to terms with the fact that we are not special, we can begin to dictate our own rules for our recovery and healing. From sobering, we transition to liberating.

This concludes Part Four. On to Part Five ...

PART FIVE

NO ONE EVER SAID THIS WAS GOING TO BE EASY

"I want to stand as close to the edge as I can without going over. Out on the edge you see all the kinds of things you can't see from the center."
—Kurt Vonnegut, *Player Piano*

24

NONLINEAR THINKING: THEY SEE FOUR, WE SEE 28

IT'S FUNNY how many of us feel that we do not belong on this planet. In late 2013, I came across an article posted on a now defunct site called Higher Perspective, titled: "Expert Claims That Humans DO NOT Come From Earth."

According to this expert, humans have a difficult time adjusting to life on earth. Giving birth is a chore, we are disease-prone, the sun tends to be our enemy, and we are synced to a 25-hour day. As for walking upright and all the back pain that goes with it, it makes far more sense that we evolved on a low-gravity planet somewhere else. Our expert raises the suggestion that aliens, possibly from Alpha Centauri, may have interbred with Neanderthals and that we are the result.

If on some level, this makes perfect sense to you, have no fear—it makes sense to me, as well. I often joke about the day when aliens will kindly abduct me and return me to the planet of my birth. Trust me, the people I confide this to laugh with me, not at me. Thus, in 2010, when I found myself telling a hundred people that "we are peanut butter people stuck in a tofu world governed by Vulcans," it was as if they had been waiting their whole lives to hear that.

Similarly, it was as if I had been waiting my whole life for their validation.

The occasion was a state Depression and Bipolar Alliance (DBSA) conference. Since I was giving this talk in Kansas, I couldn't help but bring

The Wizard of Oz into my presentation. As I explained, *The Wizard of Oz* is a movie about coming home, which is what healing is all about. Of finally—after a long long journey—arriving.

But first, Dorothy had to journey to many strange places. Weird places, crazy places, places that made no sense. As you may recall, the Yellow Brick Road didn't exactly run straight.

A major part of Joseph Campbell's hero's journey involves our universal longing to return home. We may imagine home as a physical location or a mythical place or a quiet space in our minds. Often, home is right back where we started. Something inside has shifted. We're no longer running.

The last book of the Christian Bible provides a good sense of this:

And He will wipe away every tear from their eyes; and there will no longer be any death; there will no longer be any mourning, or crying, or pain; the first things have passed away.

Screw being a Whitehall baboon in a tree, in other words. Instead, we yearn for Eden restored. It's as if our ancient tribal memory actually recalls such a place. Indeed, the first book of the Hebrew Bible lovingly describes this earthly paradise, together with the trauma of expulsion and its bitter aftermath:

By the sweat of your brow you will eat your food until you return to the ground, since from it you were taken; for dust you are and to dust you will return.

Note the Sumerian parallel. In one indelible Biblical instant, we go from plucking ripe fruit off of trees to contending with thorns and thistles. We're in Darwin's world, now—of evolution playing a practical joke on us —not to mention Freud's, of us failing to adapt to that practical joke. But this does not necessarily preclude us from lives of fulfillment, especially if we can see through the joke. Many of the people I ran into in Kansas—not to mention those in my everyday life—wear their sense of dislocation as a badge of honor.

We're not like everyone else, and thank heaven for that. With this realization comes a certain peace of mind, albeit one gained only after many wrong turns along that long and twisty Yellow Brick Road. In our differences lie our strengths. We must never confuse fitting in—living according to other people's expectations—with arriving home. Until we learn that major life lesson, we will only be tasting bitter fruit.

In this section, I will be validating this sense of disconnect, along with our feeling of not belonging. This is a theme I have dwelt on across all aspects of my writing, but this time I'm going to normalize it. Basically, before we attempt to change our behavior, we need to honor that mysterious sense of self that makes us who we are. Otherwise, all our efforts at fitting in are only going to backfire, often in a spectacular fashion.

Let me give you one example ...

A few months after my Kansas talk, I had a run-in with a friend. A certain friend of hers was being a total jerk, and the only way I could respond without making a scene was by making a scene—I left.

Naturally, my friend thought I had overreacted—made a big deal out of nothing—and from her point of view she was absolutely right. So I tried to explain what was happening from my point of view.

Such and such happened, I began, which meant such and such was going to happen. Clear as day, right?

She didn't see how my first such and such connected to my second such and such.

A light bulb went off. How could she? I reasoned. She was thinking linearly. I do, too. I have an honors law degree and highly value the power of rational thought. But many of us also seem to operate with processing units that leapfrog logic. I will be going into this in great detail in upcoming chapters. What we are looking at can best be thought of in terms of a spectrum that begins with linear thinking and progresses into nonlinear. Think of intuition as the gateway, one that bleeds into psychic perception, creativity—and madness. Connecting the extremes are circuitry and systems that not only make us highly sensitive to our environment, but have us perceiving our environment as a different reality.

Very clearly, we're living in a different world, one that can easily overwhelm us. It's as if we're experiencing reality on a quantum level, as if we are aware of the faint rustle of every individual meson and lepton. But what we sense is what we also feel, and often we feel entirely too much.

This takes us right back to where we started at the beginning of this book—to introversion. Whether we find our world a source of wonder or despair, it makes sense that we will seek out our own inner asylum. In this regard, introversion is a highly adaptive response to our often overbearing environment.

Our environment is always going to present a challenge. Always, we are flirting with depression and madness. Always, we find ourselves bruising our noses on the social brick walls that seemingly materialize out of nowhere. Far too often, our big mistake lies in assuming that our reality matches everyone else's reality.

This brings us back to my encounter with my friend, who couldn't see how my first "such and such" related to my second "such and such." Of course! How could she?

It's like this, I explained. You and your friend are thinking, "one-two-three-four." I'm already on "twenty-six, twenty-seven, twenty-eight." I already knew what was going to happen before she did.

They see four. We see twenty-eight. She thinks I'm responding inappropriately to four. Really, I'm responding as she would to 28. Probably with a lot more restraint. At least I was able to mindfully observe my brain undergoing a meltdown. At least I was able to vacate the scene before I said things that I would regret.

I wasn't asking my friend to understand me. Only that she not judge me. In effect, we occupy two different worlds. Or, rather, we see the same world through different eyes. But the hard cold reality is that the world she occupies is the one I must conform to. For every one of me or you, there are many more of her.

Let's go back to my talk at Kansas. As part of the last session of the day, I sat with a panel that fielded questions from the audience. The very first one involved bipolar and creativity. Here, I chose to frame the issue in terms of linear vs nonlinear. I informed my audience of my indebtedness to the work of Nancy Andreasen of the University of Iowa, which we will be exploring in depth in another couple of chapters.

Picking up from a remark from a presentation of hers that I had attended three years before, I noted that "our brains are organized in different ways that encourage us to think outside the box, and sometimes this means we don't test well doing linear tasks."

I went on to say:

If there's a multiple choice question, sometimes all four answers look right to me. Because in a nonlinear way, I can say, oh yeh, two plus two does equal six. Because if you do it this way and this way—can't you see that?

I looked out at a sea of nodding heads. They knew from their own experience exactly what I was talking about. I went on to explain that the people in charge of asking the questions often fail to recognize the ambiguities. They think I can't comprehend the question. My reality says they can't see that there are way too many possibilities with the answers.

This, incidentally, helps explain why for me even simple instructions may as well be written in Chinese, but for some reason I find Moby Dick light reading.

That brought us into "they see four, we see 28." As part of my own survival strategy, I explained, instead of responding with "28," I've learned to dial back my answer to six. Close enough to four make myself understood, far enough away to actually move the conversation forward.

These were the same people who had so enthusiastically embraced my remark about being peanut butter people stuck in a tofu world governed by Vulcans. To stick with peanut butter, a linear person might move to "jelly", then maybe to "bread" and stop right there—at four. We nonlinear types tend to go from "peanut butter" to "Elvis" to "ultimate universal harmonics" faster than a quark can spin.

Perhaps the linear types would have gotten there eventually. On second thought, who am I kidding? Here I am, stifling "ultimate universal harmonics" to accommodate their being still stuck somewhere between "jelly" and "bread."

For our own sanity, it pays to find our own tribe of peanut butter people, fellow outliers who understand each other. But to get along in the wider world, we also need to learn to adapt to tofu. To which one of my fellow panelists added: "The question is how do you keep from being tofu —and stay peanut butter?"

It's not always easy. Often, it involves a process of translating nonlinear thinking into linear speech. If I'm looking into questioning faces, I know I've missed my mark. That is my cue for joking in a self-deprecating way. "I have absolutely no idea what that means," I might say with perfect comedic timing in the aftermath of a bewildering universal harmonics remark. The tension eases. People are perfectly happy to accept the eccentric and quirky into their lives. But they do need to see we're attempting to meet them halfway.

Let's be clear. We all benefit from relationships with the "linear people." We need their insights and perspectives to grow and learn and to help keep us grounded. But we also need to recognize how stressful it is trying to fit in, trying to adapt to their strange folkways and customs. Inevitably, we are going to screw it up. That friend I was talking about? We never resolved the issue. Not long after, she became an ex-friend. Twenty-eight, twenty-nine, forty-two ...

25

INTUITION AND CREATIVITY

"HOW intuitive are you?" I asked in a poll on my *Knowledge is Necessity* blog at the beginning of August 2009. This came within days of my disastrous misunderstanding with my linear friend.

Intuition is generally described as "the ability to sense or know immediately without reasoning." According to journalist Hara Marano writing on *Psychology Today*:

Nonconscious processes operate all the time in complex decision-making. Often enough, we just don't give them credit. Often we cite rational-sounding criteria for our feelings and actions and do not disclose the subjective preferences of feelings that arise spontaneously.

Intuition is celebrated in our culture. We've all heard stories of the fire-fighter who senses a floor about to collapse or the art expert who spots a fake, and so on. In these situations, our man or woman of the hour is responding to subtle cues outside his or her conscious radar. But these are hardly magic powers—in all cases, our hero is operating with an expert awareness honed by years of experience.

This happens in our daily lives, as well. In traffic, for instance we're already swerving to avoid a car before we even become aware of the car or the fact that we're swerving. A lot of this can be attributed to our fight or flight circuitry. It's not always about flipping into a panic state. Recall, that our limbic and cortical regions are so tightly integrated that it is more helpful to think of them as part of the same processing unit.

In this regard, we are talking about a state of hyper-awareness that allows us to circumvent the tedious bureaucracy of thinking things through. No waiting, no lines, no filling in forms.

But what I was looking for was more like this: "My thoughts and ideas seem to come out of nowhere." Or ...

"I often read people and situations like a book." Or ...

"I can put two and two together and come up with five."

These are closer to those "aha!" moments when the mind is perfectly at rest and appears open to novel solutions. Even the hyper-rational, whether it is Newton snoozing under a tree or Sherlock Holmes playing his violin, recognize the value in switching off "thinking" and trusting in the unconscious processes of the brain.

Interesting stuff happens. Back in the eighties, a contributor to a professional journal that I edited wanted to use a pen name. No problem, I replied. I'll come up with something good. His last name was Westworth, and the article had to do with changing one's approach to a certain topic.

Hmm, I thought. This is about orientation. Orient literally means east, opposite of west. Interesting. Then I thought no more about it. A couple of days later, I woke up with the name: W.E. Stonier.

Take your time ...

Okay, time's up. Stonier is an anagram of "orients." Can you spot its opposite? Take a look at how the two initials and the first two letters in the last name combine to spell, "west." West in opposition to east, implying a shift in thinking, but also west as in preserving part of the author's name.

As elegant as Newton's laws of motion, though not nearly as significant. The point is that there is no way I could have come up with a solution as convoluted and Byzantine as this by "thinking." People who rely on their intuition to make a living say pretty much the same thing.

In a 2009 TED Talk, Elizabeth Gilbert—author of the novel, *Eat, Pray, Love*—reported that the ancient Greeks believed that creative ideas came from attendant spirits called "daemons." Socrates credited his wisdom to a daemon who spoke to him from afar. The Romans had the same idea, assigning the name "genius," to these spirits and moving them to locations inside the walls of the artist's residence or studio, sort of like Dobby the house elf.

Only during the Renaissance did the idea emerge of certain individuals "being" a genius rather than "having" a genius. But talk to any "genius," and they will be the first to tell you that they have no clue where their ideas come from. Ms Gilbert related how the poet Ruth Stone would literally feel a poem coming at her over the landscape. When this happened, the poet's priority shifted to running inside the house and grabbing pencil and paper lest the verses zoom past looking for another poet.

According to Ms Gilbert, the creative process is so demonstrably nonrational as to appear paranormal. Here's where it gets interesting. In my poll, nearly one in four answered that they were "borderline or full-on psychic, or at least it seems that way." In contrast, less than one in ten responded with, "Sorry, I'm totally rational and logical."

A classic bell curve distribution this is not. I'm guessing that most of us keep pretty quiet about this stuff, especially around our psychiatrists. After all, we are talking about a spectrum where intuition and creativity bleed into the diagnosable.

In her 1998 book *A Beautiful Mind*, author Sylvia Nasar recounts a colleague asking John Nash—the Princeton mathematician who shared the 1994 Nobel Prize in Economics—how he could believe that extraterrestrials were sending him messages.

"Because," Dr Nash replied, "the ideas that I had about supernatural beings came to me the same way that my mathematical ideas did. So I took them seriously."

Dr Nash's great creative work was done in his early-mid twenties, before his schizophrenia manifested in full. We tend to identify mental illness by severe episodes and breaks with reality, but long lead-in periods typically precede the break. Thus, during his early years, Dr Nash came across as an oddball in a profession that valued oddball thinking.

In many ways, Dr Nash's behavior paralleled that of another celebrated Princeton resident. According to Dr Andreasen, who we will feature in our next chapter, Albert Einstein was an eccentric with "schizotypal" tendencies. Schizotypy, which can be regarded as occupying the mild end of the schizophrenia spectrum, is classified as a personality disorder characterized by pronounced behavioral quirks and odd beliefs, such as in "clairvoyance, telepathy, or sixth sense."

But guess what? Creative individuals happen to test high for schizotypal tendencies. Thus, although it is bipolar that is the condition we most associate with creativity, our window into what is going on in the brain is through the schizotypy-schizophrenia spectrum.

One explanation is that those with schizotypal tendencies exhibit similar lateralization deficits as those with schizophrenia. As we discussed in an earlier chapter, this involves difficulties in handling tasks localized in the left brain, such as language. To compensate, the affected individual will recruit certain areas in the right brain. As one can imagine, this is more likely to result in some novel thinking.

Here, we are looking at a fine line between genius and madness, between inspiration and incoherency. You only have to look to Einstein's family for validation. Albert, our lovable long-haired eccentric who entertained thoughts about riding on a beam of light, came up with relativity. His son, Eduard, spent his adult life in and out of institutions.

Another explanation has to do with sensory gating. In this case, we're talking about the brain's reduced ability to filter out irrelevant noise or sensory information. For instance, if we hear someone snap his fingers twice, most of us are fairly adept in tuning out the second snap. People with schizophrenia (and some with bipolar), however, tend to process that second snap as if hearing it for the first time.

The brain is entirely too noisy for the good of its owner.

Cigarette smoking mitigates this effect, which may explain the heavy tobacco use in this population. Intriguingly, this has led to work on a "nicotine agonist" medication that may help restore quiet.

At the same time, though, research is linking our leaky filters to creativity.

The leaky filter concept comes up in discussions concerning sensory gating, but is most identified with the phenomenon of "low latent inhibition" (low LLI). Ask a random group of people, for instance, to come up with some alternative ways of using a brick (such as for a pillow), and you will find the creative and schizotypal (often one and the same) way up there in finding novel uses. The mental process is known as "divergent" thinking, where the brain free-ranges over a limitless realm of possibilities.

Of particular interest to the researchers is the precuneus, an area folded inside the parietal cortex toward the back of the brain. This region is part of the default mode network (DMN), which is most active during wakeful rest states such as daydreaming. When the brain needs to focus on a task, the precuneus, along with the rest of the DMN, fades into the background. Significantly people with schizophrenia and schizotypy experience difficulty suppressing activity in the precuneus.

As do those with creative tendencies. On one hand, we have more stimuli to work with, which is to our advantage. On the other, we can get easily overwhelmed. In this regard, all that is standing between sanity and madness is our rational capabilities.

This includes executive function, which involves the brain's ability to process information in real time and respond accordingly. People with schizophrenia face major challenges in this department, as do those of us contending with stress.

It helps to have an above average IQ. Studies have failed to find a correlation between high IQ and genius, but "high enough"—in the 120 range—appears to offer evidence of a brain capable of performing its basic cognitive tasks.

Once again, we're talking about highly integrated brain circuitry, in this case, the daydreaming parts of the brain working as one with the thinking parts. Einstein had this going for him. So, for a little while, did John Nash. Then he didn't.

The best ally, then, of the intuitive mind is the rational mind. Intuition is not to be confused with infallible wisdom. Our intuitive minds may come to stunning conclusions, but we need to avoid jumping to conclusions. Often, our intuition is just plain wrong. Our rational mind is there for a reason.

24

CREATIVITY

FROM a poem by William Blake:

*To see a world in a grain of sand/ and a heaven in a wild flower,
hold infinity in the palm of your hand/ and eternity in an hour.*

Nancy Andreasen has a rare window into the study of creativity. In the early sixties, she obtained a doctorate in literature from Oxford and joined the faculty at the University of Iowa to teach Renaissance literature. Soon after publishing a book about the poet John Donne, she entered the university's medical school and became drawn to psychiatry and neuroscience.

In the early 1970s, she joined the university's psychiatry department. There, she was told by the department's chair that her PhD in literature didn't mean shit and wouldn't count favorably toward her promotion. A quarter century later, in recognition of her pioneering research into schizophrenia and neuroimaging, she would be awarded the National Medal of Science by President Clinton. But first she had to prove her boss wrong.

Thanks to her time in the English Department, Dr Andreasen was able to recruit study subjects from the university's renowned Writer's Workshop. This included Kurt Vonnegut, who was a faculty member there during the sixties. At the time, she was exploring the anecdotal link between creativity and mental illness, and Kurt afforded an excellent case study.

Kurt battled with depression off and on. His mother committed suicide. His son, Mark, who became a successful physician and author, was originally diagnosed with schizophrenia but may actually have bipolar disorder.

Creativity also ran in the Vonnegut family. Kurt's father and grandfather were architects, his brother a chemist and inventor, his sister a sculptor, son Mark a writer, and his two daughters visual artists.

When Dr Andreasen set out to do her interviews, she expected to find reasonably well-adjusted individuals who happened to have schizophrenia in their families. For instance, a scholarly article Dr Andreasen published around that time reads: "James Joyce. Portrait of an Artist as a Schizoid." Joyce may have been only a bit weird, but his daughter spent her life as a psychiatric resident.

But instead of finding her schizophrenia connection, she told an overflowing room at the 2007 American Psychiatric Association's annual meeting in San Diego, she was "absolutely astounded" to encounter 80 percent of her subjects with some form of mood disorder, not to mention increased rates of mood disorder and creativity in their first-degree relatives.

As Dr Andreasen acknowledged: "This is a great example of starting out with the wrong hypothesis and coming up with a completely different answer."

Before we proceed any further, we need to raise the yellow caution flag. Numerous studies link bipolar to creativity, but this same research more convincingly demonstrates that the true beneficiaries are the first degree relatives. Science blogger and researcher Scott Barry Kaufman argues that these relatives—and this includes family members of those with schizophrenia—most likely inherited "a watered-down version of the mental illness," one that is "conducive to creativity while avoiding the aspects that are debilitating."

This is pretty much where Dr Andreasen is coming from as well. In her 2005 book, *The Creating Brain: The Neuroscience of Genius*, she noted that the writers she interviewed indicated that "they were unable to be creative when either depressed or manic."

Essentially, we're looking to be functional versions of our normal selves. Our own true normal, not someone else's, that magic sweet spot north of normal, south of bipolar. We need to come into our superpowers, but we also need to learn how to handle the kryptonite.

168

It was only when brain scan technology started to improve in the 1990s that Dr Andreasen considered taking the next step in her creativity research. The problem is you can't just shove a writer into a clanking MRI machine with a keyboard and wait to see what lights up on the monitor.

As she reported in an article she wrote for *The Atlantic* in 2014, after years of ruminating on what might be special about the brains of the workshop writers she had studied, she had her eureka moment: "Creative people are better at recognizing relationships, making associations and connections, and seeing things in an original way—seeing things that others cannot see."

To test for this, she needed to study the regions of the brain that go crazy when you let your thoughts wander. Her prime suspects were the association cortices (frontal, temporal, parietal, occipital). To understand how these work, first we need to recognize that that our sensory inputs are processed by highly specialized brain regions. Other specialized regions pull up memory, parse language, and so on. But none of this information makes sense in isolation, where, say, we have a visual signal walled off from a word walled off from a memory.

Enter the association cortices, which play a key role in integrating the brain's disparate sources of information. In nature, Dr Andreasen explained, we have nonlinear and dynamic self-organizing systems, where small causes may have large outcomes (think butterfly effect). Birds that take off in flight create a formation, then change places to maintain their formation. Similar dynamics can be found in the ecosystem and in the economy. No one is in charge. The whole is greater than its parts. The parts spontaneously self-organize to create something new.

Letters on a page become words, meaning is attached to them, words become connected to each other and to associated memories, which lead to richer meanings. According to Dr Andreasen, the words may be the same, but the way we make associations is what separates Shakespeare from say a stockbroker.

This time, Dr Andreasen has been recruiting scientists as well as writers and artists. Her prize catch is the film-maker George Lucas, but she also has six Nobelists and a Fields Medal mathematician. As of her 2014 *Atlantic* article, she had scanned 13 creatives along with 13 control subjects.

You cannot force creativity to happen. But you can design tasks—such as pattern recognition—that challenge the brain to make connections and solve puzzles. According to Dr Andreasen, this is the essence of the creative process. Even observing the brain at rest offers clues.

As she had hypothesized, in her creatives the association cortices ran wild. "Initially, it just might be gobbledygook," she explained. Then something locks together. Gook to gobbledygook to E=MC2. "In a way, the brain disorganizes to self-organize to produce a new idea."

Said Mozart: "Whence and how [ideas] come, I know not; nor can I force them ... Nor do I hear in my imagination the parts successively, but I hear them, as it were, all at once."

As well as performing brain scans, Dr Andreasen spent three days one-on-one with each of her celebrated creatives. This gave her an insight into their personalities. She noticed that they are adventuresome and willing to take risks. Moreover they soldier on in the face of doubt and rejection. Tellingly: "This can lead to psychic pain, which may manifest itself as depression or anxiety, or lead people to attempt to reduce their discomfort by turning to pain relievers such as alcohol."

But the reward is pure bliss. Good science, said one, "is like having good sex." Said another: "There is no greater joy that I have in my life than having an idea that's a good idea."

Her creatives informed her that their eureka moments come to them only after long periods of preparation and incubation. Typically, they occur during off-duty moments, such as in the shower, when the mind is at rest.

In addition, she observed, creative people tend to be autodidacts, people who prefer to teach themselves rather than be spoon-fed. Many also tend to be polymaths, who excel in more than one field. George Lucas, for instance, received two National Awards, one in the arts, the other in technology.

Okay, I hear you: You're not Vonnegut, you're not George Lucas. You didn't win a Nobel Prize. Not only that, your school newspaper rejected your poem for publication and people paid you good money to stop practicing your clarinet. But here's the deal: We were all born to be creative. It's part of our evolutionary toolkit. Any time you string words together into a sentence, for instance, you are engaging in the creative process. Dr Andreasen was very emphatic about this. If you have ever succeeded in talking your way out of a traffic ticket—congratulations, you have passed the basic creativity test.

To that we can add that engaging creatively with the world inside and outside of us is as much a part of the creative process as physically creating a work of art or music or literature. When you appreciate the beauty of a tree in nature, congratulations, you have experienced that tree as no one has ever experienced it before. Not only that, many of us inhabit deep and rich interior worlds that have nothing to do with the ability to express ourselves. Our sense of wonder remains valid, even if words fail us.

Often they do.

27

THE PARANORMAL, SPIRITUALITY, AND THE UNCONSCIOUS MIND

ON A BLOG at *HealthCentral*, I posed this question to my readers:

This happened to me back in the mid-70s: I had a vivid dream about an earthquake, so vivid that upon awakening I mentioned it to my then wife. Next morning the ground shook, my first earthquake experience.

Question: Anything psychic or paranormal or bordering on such ever happen to you? Maybe it wasn't out of the ordinary. Maybe it was simply a zillion-to-one coincidence. Call it what you want. Tell us all about it and don't be shy.

"We're called nut jobs for recounting these experiences", Liza replied, "and don't you dare mention them to your psychiatrist unless you want a stay in a psych ward complete with an ECT session or two."

Nevertheless, Liza felt sufficiently safe to reveal this:

I was in a small group in my high school English class. The group was discussing the debate we were preparing, and I said, why are we going over this again? We said all this at our last small-group meeting. Nope. It was the first time we'd met in group. My classmates already thought I was weird, and I'd just confirmed it.

172

Liza ventured that mania helps bring on intuitive insight, but that two memorable prescient dreams she experienced had nothing to do with mania. Another reader volunteered that most of her psychic and paranormal experiences are enhanced by mania. But another cautioned that: "When I have been psychotic I have thought I was having lots of paranormal experiences, so this is one I just can't touch. I'd be in to see my doctor if I thought I was having a psychic experience. Sorry guys."

Just so we're clear: In my first book in this series, I recounted the experience of Maricela Estrada, who had a vision of the end of the world and stripped off her blouse in public to be as naked as Adam and Eve. She was driven off in a police car, handcuffed, with breasts exposed.

This was florid psychosis, pure and simple. Maricela had the courage to disclose her humiliation and trauma in her 2009 book, *Bipolar Girl*. She is a mental health hero who is doing well now, and has been honored by the National Alliance on Mental Illness (NAMI). Maricela credits her religious faith as being vital to her in her recovery, but she would be the last to confuse a psychotic experience with a religious or spiritual one.

There is no sugar-coating breakdowns of this magnitude, no looking for possible adaptive advantages, no romanticizing. John Nash's 1994 Nobel honored him for work he produced four decades earlier, when he was in his twenties, when he merely exhibited schizotypal traits. Then his brain quit on him. In his Nobel biography, Dr Nash refers to a "gap period of about 25 years of partially deluded thinking" which provided "a sort of vacation."

But when is a delusion not a delusion? Suppose, for instance, you recall as a kid distinctly having seen a faint luminous figure, head detached, floating out of your mother's room? Even if you are convinced of the veracity of your recollection, chances are you will be very careful who you disclose this to. Certainly not your psychiatrist. Certainly not the entire world.

Believe it or not, none other than a psychiatrist had this vision. Not only that, he revealed it to the entire world. In addition, he fully documented his own mental breakdown as an adult, together with the lengthy period of emotional anguish that followed.

If you are guessing this had to be Carl Jung, founder of analytic psychiatry, you are correct. Jung felt that the human psyche is "by nature religious," and he spent much of his life investigating eastern and related philosophies, which influenced his take on personal healing—individuation —as the reconciliation of opposites, the yin with the yang.

None of this, of course, sat well with his mentor Freud, who described the Catholic faith as "the enemy" and who expressed his fear of psychiatry descending into a "black tide of mud of occultism." Jung, in the meantime, had serious misgivings about science as the new dogma, divorced from inner spiritual experience.

In 1913, following an acrimonious split with Freud, Jung suffered a breakdown in which he expressed fear that he was "doing a schizophrenia," which he also referred to as "a confrontation with the unconscious." He recalled, "I often had to cling to the table, so as not to fall apart." On the lake shore in Zurich he collected stones and built a miniature village, including a castle, cottages, and a church.

In 1914, sufficiently recovered, he set aside time to deliberately cultivate that state of mind when things fell apart on him. This involved settling into a meditative rest state and having conversations with the beings who entered his inner awareness.

One of these was "Philemon," who personified an ancient universal wisdom. More often, though, he faced creatures who represented his own dark side. For instance: "I hear steps on the stairway, the steps creak, he knocks: a strange fear comes over me: there stands the red one, his long shape wholly shrouded in red ..."

Over a period of 16 years, Jung recorded his impressions in a journal which became known as *The Red Book*. The insights he gained from these experiences formed the basis of his psychiatry. For decades after his death, his book sat hidden in a bank vault, not available to the public. Its eventual publication in 2009 proved to be a revelation—the pages are hand-lettered in a medieval Gothic script, replete with stylized capitals and accompanied by illuminated illustrations.

Many of the illustrations portray archetypal beings in phantasmagorical settings featuring objects and symbols laden in mystical meanings. Other times, the illustrations are purely abstract, with stylized mandalas or Celtic crosses or splashes of color arranged into kaleidoscopic fractals.

According to the *Guardian*: "The book is a remarkable blend of calligraphy and art; an illuminated manuscript that bears comparison with *The Book of Kells* and William Blake."

If you are thinking that Jung may have accessed a type of deep trance state we associate with Christian and Eastern mystics and shamanic practitioners, you definitely have a point. To understand this, we need to take a closer look at the brain's default mode network (DMN), which we made brief reference to in an earlier chapter.

The DMN refers to discrete but linked cortical regions that are most active when we are experiencing wakeful rest. When engaged in performing a task, though, a different network becomes dominant, the task positive network (TPN). Believe it or not, until the publication of a 2001 study by Marcus Raischle of Washington University (St Louis), hardly anyone even suspected the brain was organized this way.

In the past, if you were investigating the neural basis to any particular human behavior, standard operating procedure was to perform a scan while engaging the subject in some sort of cognitive task (such as trying to decipher a simple visual puzzle), then seeing which circuits lit up. When Dr Raischle noted that certain areas of the brain seemed to come on line as his subjects were resting between tasks, he decided to take a closer look.

According to Dr Raischle: "It hadn't occurred to anyone that the brain is actually just as busy when we relax as when we focus on difficult tasks."

Observing the brain at rest led to the discovery of the DMN, but it took several years before it became a hot research field. *Wikipedia* states that prior to 2007, there were but 12 published papers that mentioned the DMN. Between 2007 and 2014, we had nearly 1,400. A quick *PubMed* search reveals that the first DMN study involving bipolar was only published in 2010.

With a field of inquiry this new, we need to acknowledge that a good many study findings will be tentative, at best, no matter how rigorously researched, and that any attempts to generalize necessarily involves a good deal of speculation. Nevertheless, a picture is emerging of a dynamic and fluid brain network that seems to shift in and out of various states according to the laws of quantum physics.

We start with the proposition that this network is most active during our resting state. But here's the catch. The circuitry is far more dense than those parts of the brain we associate with performing tasks and is metabolically far more active. This means a lot more is going on than simply the brain idling in neutral. As more studies get published, we are discovering that the DMN is associated with our own internal dialogues, that these dialogues are vital to our sense of self, and that without this sense of self, the tasks we perform have no reference point.

That's about as deep as we can get, but there's more. It seems that our ability to time travel—to learn from the past and imagine the future, to just plain imagine—zips and zooms along these circuits. Thus, instead of blindly reacting to our immediate environment, we are more cogently responding through our accumulated wisdom and experience. Likewise, we can employ our powers of imagination to anticipate our future and plan ahead.

Not only that, our "theory of mind" appears to derive from the DMN. This refers to our ability to employ our higher sense of self-awareness as a tool in recognizing the mental states of others.

Thus, if we are ever to identify a seat of conscious, it is most likely to be found in the constantly shifting neural connections within the DMN. Significantly, the regions of the brain fingered in Alzheimers correspond to deficits in the regions in the DMN. In this regard, we may think of Alzheimers as not only a loss of memory, but a loss of identity.

We are also discovering the DMN is heavily implicated in depression. This has to do with the proposition that our own internal dialogues may give rise to unhealthy ruminating, self-criticism, and incessant worries over the past and future.

When those around us tell us to "snap out of it," well now we have a brain science explanation for what they would like to see happen. In effect, they want us to flip our switch from the DMN to the TPN, from the internal morass we are mired in to active engagement in our external world. This, of course, is easier said than done, which strongly implies the need for research into treatments and therapies that would facilitate making the switch.

Coincidentally, new studies into psychedelic drugs are yielding invaluable insights into where to look. Compounds such as LSD first came to the attention of clinicians and researchers in the 1950s as a possible means to help patients see beyond the constraints of their narrow ego identities. With the hippie drug culture of the sixties, however, came the inevitable political reaction. The net effect was a virtual shutdown of research for the next four decades.

Now, we are beginning to see a reboot in the research. One drug of interest includes psilocybin, which occurs naturally from "magic" mushrooms and which enhances serotonin transmission. One effect of the drug is that both the DMN and TPN get turned down. This represents a stark contrast to business as usual, where one mode is expected to phase in while the other phases out. Intriguingly, the very opposite happened when researchers scanned the brains of Tibetan Buddhist monks as they meditated. In this case, the DMN and TPN simultaneously got turned up.

Not surprisingly, when something as out of the ordinary as this happens, the brain is going to have a different experience with reality. Those who have used psilocybin or engaged in deep meditation or, for that matter, simply been struck out of the blue by a sudden shift in awareness talk about arriving at inner knowing, experiencing a disintegration of the ego, and achieving a profound sense of connection.

According to William James in his classic *The Varieties of Religious Experience*: "In mystic states we both become one with the Absolute and we become aware of our oneness."

The experience is typically short, no longer than about 30 minutes, but the effect may stay with the person the rest of his or her life. Indeed, the event is likely to be recalled decades later as life-changing.

Could our altered states provide insights into the hidden forces that influence our our more mundane behavior? According to Robin Cathart-Harris of Imperial College, who has been using psylocibin to investigate the DMN, in the past our only windows into the unconscious have been via dreams and psychotic states. The use of psychedelics in research, he claims, may shed light on that which is latent in the mind.

In this regard, we hear echoes of Dr Kandel's call for a new science of the mind, one that would integrate Freud with neuroscience. Essentially, Freud was onto something when he came up with the idea of the unconscious mind. It's just that for the longest time we had no credible explanation—nothing to point to—to validate its existence.

Now Dr Cathart-Harris and his colleagues feel reasonably confident in proposing "the entropic brain hypothesis," which imagines our consciousness along a broad spectrum ranging from high disorder flexible states (think of something fluid) to low disorder rigid states (think of something solid), with our normal waking conscious in the middle.

Is there a place in this spectrum for realities existing beyond our normal conscious states? Jung certainly thought this was worth looking into when he induced his own meditative trances. His *Red Book* offers clear physical evidence of what we can achieve when we leave ourselves open to whatever our own inner awareness may reveal.

But we also need to be mindful of the fact that many of us already seem to live inside a much wider mental and sensory and emotional bandwidth than what may be good for us. In this regard, one can be forgiven for simply wanting to turn down the volume. Heaven knows, last thing I need is vivid earthquake dreams, especially living in California.

In the realm of the psychic and spiritual, psychosis is always lurking in the background, ready at the slightest opportunity of bursting into the foreground. We may indeed have rare gifts. But we need to be careful. Being reduced to a life of eating out of dumpsters should not be the price we pay for acquiring a deeper awareness.

NONLINEAR

Intuition   Creativity

Alternate   Psychosis,
Reality   BP, SZ

The overlap is self-evident.

28

DECONSTRUCTING INTROVERSION

LET'S BRING introversion back into the discussion. As you recall from Part One of this book, my introversion is complicit in my depressions. If I'm not careful, my preference for being alone in my own thoughts can lead to a dangerous tendency to isolate, to literally give up on being a social animal. More than once, my brain has responded by shutting down.

I also related how my introversion played an ironic role in the making of one memorable manic episode that rendered me unemployable. In that instance, over a seven or eight-month period, I overcompensated for my introversion by willing myself to succeed in a job that demanded a high level of social interaction. On that occasion, my brain responded by flipping out.

Thus, we have a classic case of how an underlying personality "trait" can lead to a mood "state." Simply knowing that we have bipolar is not enough. Whether it's introversion or something else, our natural tendencies to default to certain behaviors over others have a way of setting the scene for those depressions and manias that seemingly come out of nowhere. If only it were just bipolar.

Introversion was my gateway into appreciating the link between mood and personality. If you identify as an extravert, trust me—this chapter applies to you, as well. There's a lot more going on than meets the eye. I began to develop an insight into this back in 2003, when one of my website readers raised the issue of whether our Myers-Briggs personality types bore any relation to bipolar. Hmm, I thought.

The Myers-Briggs Type Indicator (MBTI) is an immensely popular personality test. Numerous self-tests can be found all over the web. The scientific validity of the MBTI has been called into question, but this shouldn't stop you from using it as a rough guide for developing insights into your own behavior. If you want to have a friendly conversation with another person comparing test scores, by all means go ahead. But please do not judge others based on these labels.

Fortunately, the MBTI has no built-in value judgments. This is in sharp contrast to psychology's signature personality test, the Five Factor Model (FFM), which not only regards extraversion as preferable to introversion, but views the latter as a sort of pathology, to be lumped with other negative traits such as lack of agreeableness and neuroticism.

The person who would most strenuously object to this, by the way, would be the one who came up with introversion and extraversion in the first place, none other than Carl Jung. Jung, of course, led the type of deep and imaginative and reflective inner life that lends itself so readily to introversion. It is difficult to imagine, for instance, an extravert producing their own *Red Book*.

Jung's take on how we tend to view the world in different ways (such as thinking vs feeling) served as the model for the MBTI. Like so many of us picking up the pieces in the wake of a personal disaster (in this case, being ostracized by Freud), Jung was trying to make sense of his life. So it was that I followed up on my reader's suggestion by asking subscribers to my email newsletter to take an online MBTI test and send me the results, along with their diagnosis.

My first jaw-dropping finding was that eight in 10 of my respondents identified as introverts. Among the general population, by contrast, studies place introverts in the clear minority, at anywhere from one-quarter to less than one-half of the general population.

Had this been a scientific study, of course, I would have made sure all my respondents were in remission from depression and mania before they took the test. Had that been the case, it is likely that my findings would have replicated those of other studies that find extraverts in the majority of the bipolar population. But "normal" is merely one phase in our mood cycles. We are depressed way more than manic, and a good many of us are depressed way more than "normal."

This is important because extraversion-introversion is changeable with mood, not set in stone. As one of my respondents remarked: "When manic I'm as sociable as Bette Midler on cocaine and when I'm depressed, seriously come not near me." Another wrote that eight years before, when he took the test at work in a stimulating environment, he was an extravert, but at home where he could relax away from people he was an introvert.

So maybe my informal survey represents the truer picture, namely that introversion is far more prevalent in our population than conventional wisdom would have us believe.

At the time, I was beginning to connect my tendency to isolate to my depressions, so I was hardly looking at introversion as an enviable characteristic. In a pair of journal articles I came across, David Janowsky of UNC fingered isolation as a risk factor for suicidality and noted that "increased introversion predicts the persistence of depressive symptoms and a lack of remission."

This led me to conclude at the time that our best protection against depression is to get out the door and socialize more often. I can't emphasize how vital this is to our well-being. Nevertheless, I was only seeing half the picture. By 2009, I was beginning to entertain notions of a positive side to introversion, but my thinking only began to crystallize toward the end of 2010.

The precipitating event involved the sweeping changes that the American Psychiatric Association was considering making to a portion of its diagnostic bible, the DSM. Part of this included incorporating a modified version of the FFM as a template for assessing personality disorders.

Thus, the first draft of the DSM-5 highlighted "introversion" as a pathology, along with "negative emotionality" and "antagonism."

This led one of my blog readers, Jill, who identified as an introvert, to comment: "What's concerning me is that it suggests the psychiatrists of the world have decided we need to be a nation of Rotarians."

Not that there's anything wrong with being a Rotarian, mind you, but it's fair to say that psychology and psychiatry—reflecting the views of society-at-large—value sociability over over personal reflection, superficial social connections over deep thinking, pat answers over nuanced problem-solving, and conformity over breaking the mold.

Off the top of my head, George W Bush—the second-worst President in US history after James Buchanan—would be psychiatry's ideal extravert poster boy. Something is truly very wrong with this picture.

"Can an extravert do my job?" I asked in a blog on *HealthCentral*. The work I do involves long hours in isolation, blotting out all distractions, researching and writing about mental illness and behavior. For a major project, this may involve shutting myself off for days at a stretch, with days occasionally turning into weeks.

How does an extravert handle these situations? Not too well. As Jill reports on her younger sister:

She dies a thousand deaths each night she is alone. She lives for companionship and would almost rather be with the wrong person than to be alone. She is either on the phone or with someone or planning her next outing—all the time. ... And when she is alone, she feels abandoned.

If we were to seek an ideal, it would be in a best-of-both-worlds scenario, with people capable of changing emphasis from one to the other, from being a self-assured glad-hander to a thoughtful loner and back again, as the situation demands. These are your "ambiverts," people who can hold their own in numerous settings, whether working as part of a team or flying solo.

We also need to have regard for the fact that absolutes are a rarity. With introversion and extraversion, we tend to lean in one direction or the other, but we're not necessarily frozen in place. With practice, we can acquire a bit more flexibility, but the effort will always suck energy out of us, and this is the point: Introverts come alive inside their own thoughts, extraverts from other people.

By way of a personal example, on those occasions I do get out of the house, I may unaccountably perk up around people. This happens only when I feel comfortable. Otherwise, at gatherings, I'm the one you will find off in a distant corner, communing with the cheese dip. But when I am at ease, some of my exuberant tendencies will kick in and I may—of all things—find myself the life of the party.

People who have only seen me in these situations would mistake me for an extravert. If they rode home with me, however, they would see me crashing to earth, too spent to stop off and run any errands I may have planned. My psychic battery is drained, no gas in the tank. Nothing, entropy. At this stage, my pressing survival need is asylum, sanctuary, peace and quiet.

With extraverts, of course, it's an entirely different story. It's not that we can't lead successful lives in their world. But we do need to know how to pace ourselves.

Richard Nixon, 37th President of the US, affords an excellent case study. According to Tom Wicker, political columnist at the *New York*

Times back in the sixties through the eighties: "Richard Nixon was an introvert in the extraverted calling of the politician."

Let us pause for a second to ponder the sheer improbability of a man who came across as a fish out of water, socially awkward, with cartoonish mannerisms, somehow gaining the trust of enough voters to elevate him to the most powerful person on earth. According to one account, our introvert-in-chief arranged it so that at formal White House dinners he would talk to "as few people as possible," and that no conversation would last more than five minutes.

For a quick contrast, the man he ran against in 1968, Hubert Humphrey, was known as "the Happy Warrior."

Yet, those close to Nixon describe him as thoughtful and engaging in private, with a powerful intellect. These are qualities that would have taken him high in law or academia, social awkwardness and all, without the burdens of overextending himself in public.

In 1952, it appeared his political career was about to come to a precipitous and ignominious end. In the wake of press reports of a personal slush fund, Nixon found himself under pressure to step down as Eisenhower's Vice Presidential running mate. He responded by booking 30 minutes of TV time and delivering the speech of his life. This included a personal anecdote about a new dog named Checkers—hence the "Checkers Speech." By the end of his presentation, the camera man was in tears. A vast flood of telegrams poured in, 75 to one in his favor.

Believe it or not, introverts can be formidable in public. Part of this has to do with the infinite preparation we are willing to put in beforehand, alone, inside our own thoughts. Nixon was the type of person who lived for being in a quiet space, parsing complex issues, and scribbling into his yellow legal pads. This was how he prepared his Checkers speech, spending two days in seclusion, only divulging his thoughts to his wife and two advisers.

When he faced the camera, it was evident the hard work paid off. His presentation was nothing short of formidable. Moreover, he spoke to an empty room, with no fear of being thrown off his game by the vagaries of a live audience. With his career on the line, to an introvert, even a friendly crowd would have been stressful.

But we all know, that over the long term, this story had no happy ending, and here we can make a strong case that introversion played a major role in his ultimate downfall and disgrace. His character flaws have been well-documented. If introverts tend to live inside their own thoughts, Nixon was cursed with some peculiarly strange and dark ones. Here, it is safe to speculate that his sense of isolation not only fed his demons but silenced any distress signals. Deep inside your walled-off inner world, no one senses the hells you endure.

Ironically, in his new incarnation as a disgraced ex-President, Nixon may have found a certain inner peace that had eluded him all his life. After an initial period of bad health, financial insecurity, and depression, he settled into the type of calling that best matched his talents and temperament—that of thinker-at-large. Now he could shut himself off in his quiet spaces with his yellow legal pads and scribble to his heart's content.

From his quiet spaces came a wealth of think pieces, including ten books, numerous articles, and the type of speeches he could deliver on his own terms, to receptive audiences. The world outside his door became a much friendlier place. This time, he could aspire to a more noble calling—being himself.

After a lifetime of struggle, our introvert had come home.

29

THE IDEALIST, THE HIGHLY SENSITIVE PERSON, THE EMPATH, AND THE ALTRUIST

WE'RE BACK to my email newsletter survey, where I asked my readers to take an online MBTI test and email the results. As I related in the previous chapter, my first jaw-dropping finding was that eight in ten of my respondents tested for introversion. This can best be explained by the fact that introversion-extraversion can shift with mood, with the high likelihood that a good many of my respondents were depressed at the time.

My second jaw-dropping finding had to do with my respondents clustering around a few rare personality types. In this case, research turned into me-search. Let me explain ...

My own MBTI retesting confirmed my profile from years before. "INFP" was my type—one of 16 possibilities—alias "questor" or "dreamer." The "I" in INFP stands for introvert.

Basically, leave me in a cave in Tibet for ten years, with occasional weekends off, and I'll be just fine. As you may guess, we INFPs are a fairly rare breed, comprising but two percent of the general population. So when a bunch of INFP results started to roll in, I got pretty excited. Out of the first 100 replies I tabulated, 14 were my people. Just one letter off, an equally rare breed the INFJs—"mystics"—constituted an eye-opening 17 percent.

Also, just one letter off were ENFPs—visionaries—at seven percent the only group of extraverts over-represented in my survey.

Think about it: Thirty-eight mystics and dreamers and visionaries—clear outsiders—in an imaginary room where one would expect to find only four or five or six. But in a largely bipolar and depressed population, the outsiders turned out to be close to the norm. What on earth was going on?

Okay, first let's break down the alphabet soup. We know the "I" in INFP stands for introversion (as opposed to extraversion). The N signifies intuition (as opposed to sensing), the F for feeling (as opposed to thinking), and the P for perceiving (as opposed to judging).

In our imaginary room of people with depression and bipolar, it is reasonable to expect that intuitives and feelers would be over-represented, and this proved to be the case (by a two-thirds majority for each). It's not that intuitives lack the ability to stay grounded or that feelers don't think. Like everything else about behavior, we're talking about tendencies rather than absolutes.

Moreover, if we think of bipolar as a condition where we think and feel and perceive wider and deeper than the rest of the population, even if we identify as "feelers" we're also certainly engaged in a lot of deep thinking—more so, I would submit, than most of those in the general population who identify as thinkers.

Where it starts to get interesting is when we officially join up these two middle letters in our four-letter combinations. Three of these combinations (such as S for sensing and T for thinking) yield fairly mainstream temperaments: Artisans (concrete and adaptable), guardians (concrete and organized), rationals (abstract and objective).

When we come to our tribe of mystics and dreamers and visionaries, though, we seem to form our own unique outlier class of "idealist" intuitives and feelers (NFs). What we lack in terms of fitting in we make up for in passion and commitment. Four in ten in my sample turned up as idealists.

THE IDEALISTS

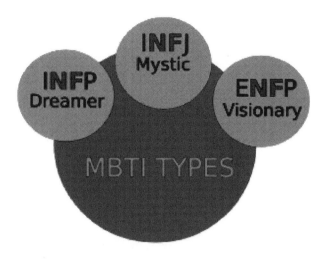

In the MBTI, those with NF (intuitive-feeler) inclinations represent "Idealists." Note, also, the "I" for introversion. Both introverts and Idealists were way over-represented in my depression-bipolar sample. Idealists also roughly correspond to being "highly sensitive," as well as having a high capacity for empathy. In addition, we can make a strong case that these people are also inclined to think non-linearly, with intuitive and creative gifts, plus display the ability to access alternate states of mind. In this regard, we have a special outlier class of individuals who perceive reality a good deal differently than the more mundane majority.

Back in 2003, when I first wrote about this on my website, I did not fully appreciate the merits of being way out on the idealist fringe. At the time, I was emerging from a lengthy period of social isolation and was trying to fit in to the "normal" majority. It took Greg, one of my readers, to call me out.

"A point that seems to be missed," he commented, "is that mystics and dreamers are not like the other 99 percent of the population because we DO see a different perspective and that our depression stems from the inability to relate to the general values of the mass population."

These include, he went on to say, "obnoxious, self-centered narcissists who have little respect for topics which do not serve them in some way."

People with our tendencies, he asserted, become depressed after years of being surrounded by our simple-minded sports and pop culture. Thus: "To view us as bipolar or ill in some way is to miss the simple point that we ARE NOT like others and do not want to be."

Greg was only just getting warmed up. Here's his money paragraph:

The advice that we would be better off somehow by getting out more often and mingling with the very people we can't relate to makes no sense at all. Should I wish to go to a bar and watch the game along with a bunch of egotistical good old boys while they unconsciously stuff hamburgers into their faces and root for some overpaid moron running with a ball? Are we really an advanced civilization?

I stay away from these people because they disgust me. Otherwise, I may as well get a lobotomy and become a rancher who owns a baseball team—or a logger that cuts down natural habitats so I can ship logs to Japan, or perhaps a lobbyist for the insurance industry who can keep people from affording healthcare. No, it's not the Idealists who are sick— we're just the ones pointing out the sickness.

I'm embarrassed to admit how long it took me to fully appreciate where Greg was coming from. Back then, he and I may not have had much to talk about. I like to think over the years that I've grown, that I've become more like him. Heaven help that he became more like me.

Perhaps we can better understand ourselves by approaching our Idealist tendencies from the perspective of "the highly sensitive person." In her 1997 book, *The Highly Sensitive Person: How to Thrive When the World Overwhelms You*, Elaine Aron observes that many of us are so highly attuned to the subtleties in our surroundings that we are easily overwhelmed to the point of exhaustion. Dr Aron, herself a card-carrying "HSP," reports that we notice far more than mere objects in the room. Not surprisingly, we tend to be gifted in the usual creative and insightful and emotional ways. But, like our other gifts, it comes at a steep price, one that invites misunderstanding and ridicule. Life is a challenge, and because of this we easily find ourselves marginalized by the less sensitive majority.

In a blog on *Mental Health Talk*, writer Rachel Miller reports:

I've always felt like an outsider, so different to everybody else, like I had been dropped off on the wrong planet. Everyone around me, even at primary school, seemed so settled in the world, like living on Earth was the easiest and most natural thing. I felt alien.

See. It's not just me. It's as if none of us belong here. What's wrong with the people on this planet?

Phil Ochs is probably the most influential folk singer/political activist you never heard of. His story is lovingly yet unsentimentally captured on the 2010 documentary film by Ken Bowser, *Phil Ochs: There but for Fortune*.

In 1962, fresh out of Ohio, Ochs arrived on the Greenwich Village folk music scene when it was in full flower. Kennedy had been in office for a year, and his New Frontier held out the promise of the full unlocking of human potential. Whatever wrongs there were in the world could be righted. It was a new day.

Very quickly, Ochs found his voice as a singing journalist, performing his own wry musical commentaries on the events of the day, part of a scene that included Pete Seeger, Peter, Paul, and Mary, Joan Baez, and Bob Dylan. His first album, in 1964 for Elektra Records, was titled, *All the News That's Fit to Sing*.

Dylan and Ochs initially had a friendly rivalry going. Indeed, Ochs aspired to be a Dylan, but the only way to do that would have been to pen his own "Blowin' in the Wind."

Although mass market success eluded Ochs, he was at the epicenter of a movement that deeply resonates half a century later. Phil and his guitar were everywhere—at music gigs, at folk festivals, at political protests. Deeper into the sixties, change was still possible, but this time it was more like pushing a rock uphill. A martyred President ended our innocence. The Vietnam War escalated. Pent-up racial frustrations erupted on the streets. King was assassinated. RFK was assassinated. Too many martyrs. Political opinion polarized and hardened. An unenlightened reaction set in. Richard Nixon assumed the Presidency having cynically pandered to the prejudices of his "great silent majority."

The protest movement fragmented and headed off on its course of self-destruction.

As *There but for Fortune* makes loud and clear, Phil took all this far more personally than everyone else. The cover to his 1969 album, *Rehearsals for Retirement*, says it all. We see his own tombstone, announcing his death in Chicago, 1968, scene of epochal anti-war demonstrations that Ochs helped organize. As Richard O'Connor in *Undoing Depression* remarked:

I can't help thinking that part of the reason was the pain his vision cost him—the pain of putting yourself in the place of the "other guy," of not allowing yourself to feel safe and superior to a faceless, anonymous other, but knowing except for a few lucky breaks you might be in that position yourself.

Dr O'Connor was referring to Ochs' capacity for empathy—the ability to walk in the shoes of others, to the point of identifying with their suffering, even with total strangers. It's one of the crowning achievements of the human condition, but it's a mixed blessing. An over-tendency to empathize may lead to depression, and the man who symbolically killed himself in 1968 several years later did it for real. He was 36.

You might describe empathy as the mirror opposite of sociopathy and narcissism. Indeed, the sociopath and the narcissist have serious issues expressing true empathy. It's as if they are wired that way. The most credible biological explanation for empathy has to do with "mirror neurons," located in the frontal lobes. In studies done on monkeys, researchers found that certain regions of the brain would light up in response to whatever the other monkey was doing, such as ripping up paper. The response would mirror the brain activity of the other monkey in every way except for those neural systems that governed movement.

In other words, the observer monkey was responding as if it were ripping up its own piece of paper, even though it was doing no such thing.

Our singular ability to identify with others—including their suffering—sets the scene for altruism. On the face of it, this type of behavior runs so counter to our own basic survival needs that even those who are not sociopaths and narcissists find themselves scratching their heads. Yes, we fully understand how parents willingly put their child's needs above their own. And we also have a passing appreciation of tribal identity and the manifold advantages that can accrue from putting the group's interests above our own.

On top of that, we seem to have an intuitive grasp of the benefits of maintaining a healthy karmic balance sheet, not to mention a practical feel for doing unto others.

We are social animals, after all. This stuff isn't rocket science.

But taking the principle of altruism a step or two farther tends to baffle us. Even as we honor the Good Samaritans and humanitarians in our midst, even as we reflect on those who made the ultimate sacrifice—even as two billion of us worldwide celebrate a being who willingly suffered and died that all of us may live—something in us says it can't be real. The rational among us will tell you that altruism is built with its own inherent contradiction—that even the most selfless and sublime action has to be rooted in some deep-seated self-interest.

I would hardly dispute this. I would simply argue that there exists a rare breed who possess that singular gift of finding a self-interest where none seemingly exists, together with the ability to join it to a mission or life purpose that makes no sense to anyone else.

Who are these people? Perhaps you have already figured it out. They are the nonlinear amongst us, the ones who see 28 where others see only four. They are the intuitives and creatives, capable of pulling novel ideas and imaginative solutions out of thin air. They are the other-worldly, who possess the uncommon ability to tap into a different reality.

Each characteristic seems to blend into the other, and this includes madness. Madness (including depression) may be lurking in the shadows or it may reveal itself in all its DSM horror. Whatever the case, a good many of us have managed to reach an accommodation, however fragile. Even if to an outsider, our lives appear to be nothing more than a constant succession of train-wrecks, a good many of us have found a certain level of comfort deep inside our improbably wired brains. We have made a home there. We have somehow reconciled a thousand contradictions between the expectations of our often indifferent or hostile social peers and our own confounding sensibilities.

Wait—there's more ...

Here's to the introverts, built for self-reflection and deep-thinking. Here's to the idealists—mystics, dreamers, and visionaries—born to march to a different drummer. Here's to the highly sensitive, equipped with different radar, who react to things that are seemingly not there. And finally the empaths, with the rare capacity to walk in the shoes of others.

Again, one quality bleeds into the other. Again, madness is a constant traveling companion. But madness is a two-way street—a psychiatric Shiva— as much a creator as a destroyer, a shaper of personalities as well as the wrecking ball.

THE OUTLIERS

Intuitive/Creative · Other-worldly · Madness · Empath · Sensitive · Idealist · Introvert · Nonlinear

To this outlier class of individuals, the extraordinary is perfectly ordinary, the ordinary extraordinary. Say what you want about adaptation being the key to survival, George Bernard Shaw had an answer for this. "The reasonable man," he wrote, "adapts himself to the world; the unreasonable one persists in trying to adapt the world to himself. Therefore all progress depends on the unreasonable man."

How unreasonable is altruism? It is a concept so absurd and ridiculous that what is an anathema to the sociopath and narcissist and what at best makes limited sense to the commendably rational is going to come across as self-evident to a good many of us. So much so that we intuitively grasp the paradox that we best serve ourselves by freely and willingly serving others.

"Service to others," said Muhamad Ali, "is the rent you pay for your room here on earth."

And therein lies the key to the puzzle. Home is all around us. Wherever we reach out to serve others—that is the place where we truly belong. The planet we were born to live on is the one whose fellow beings we ultimately find ourselves embracing.

Four billion years in a series of accidents have led us here. If there is a purpose to the peculiar accident that we call life, it lies in finding meaning.

We find meaning in freely serving others. Really—it's as simple as that. You may not "get it" right now, but thanks to your own unique cluster of outlier qualities, you are wired to make the realization when the time is right.

Within our deepest vulnerabilities lie our greatest gifts. Our lifelong search for identity takes on new meaning. Our fate may be the road less traveled, one that involves endless travails along numerous trails of tears, but it leads us to places we dare not ever have imagined. Out of the darkness—a distant gleam. We pick ourselves off the ground and take a tentative step forward. Then a more confident step. Then—when the time is right—a leap. A bold leap, a leap of faith, a leap into the unknown.

Four billion years of evolution have prepared us for this journey.

At long last, we are on our way home ...

CLOSING MEDITATION

THE WORLD (bathtubs with
feet). That's the only thing that
makes sense, nowadays.

Maybe someday
Maybe someday

Maybe someday ...

Aliens will kindly
abduct me and return me
to the planet of my birth.

Da-di-da-rong-dong-dong
Da-di-da-rong-dong-dong
Da-diddlee-dop da-diddlee-dop
Da diddlee-dop-dup!

I had a nightmare
that I danced like a white man.
I wake up. Oh shit!

The world (bathtubs with feet) ...

Not easy being

illogical. Spock does not
understand peanut butter.

Tup-it-tah tup-it-tah tup-it-tah dong-dong
Tup-it-tah tup-it-tah tup-it-tah dong-dong

I perform my own
stunts. Leaping, stumbling, cursing,
gritting my teeth through the pain.

Learning as I go
along. Sisyphus rolls
his rock. Splat!

The world (bathtubs with feet) ...

Dup-dup!

I am being pulled
into the abyss. Wait! I'm
lifting someone out of the mire.

My load is heavy,
my burden light. Crazy,
I know. Crazy, crazy.

Something funny just happened ...

I know a place
filled with shady trees
and people with picnic baskets.

Shakti, she beckons,
Kwan Yin, Sophia, Isis.
Join us, on our blanket.

Thai noodles, yogurt
and cilantro. Mmm, juicy
watermelon chunks.

The world (bathtubs with
feet). I am safe. And welcome.
I am—I am home.

Did-arong dah-rong da-rong da-rong
Did-arong dah-rong da-rong da-rong
Did-arong did
Di doddle-dup di doddle-dup di doddle-doddle-dup!

POSTSCRIPT

IN MAY 2016, I set aside work on this book to attend to another project. In mid-July, a week or so away from returning to these pages, I experienced severe shortness of breath, chest pain, and a tingling in my upper left arm.

I called my brother, who drove me to the nearest ER. I was half-expecting to be sent home with a baby Aspirin. Three days later, a highly dedicated medical team cracked me open like a lobster and performed quadruple bypass surgery.

By rights, my heart should have stopped beating months before. It was totally blocked, and my cardiologist had images to prove it. I had been breathing on borrowed time. Had I not called my brother, had he not picked up the phone, it never would have occurred to me to call 911. I'm guessing, then, I would have been down to my last or second-to-last sunset.

In the past, I have characterized suicidal depression as a heart attack of the brain. Everything inside shuts down. Your life is hanging by a thread. Now, actually having survived both a severe cardiac crisis and a suicidal depression, I can attest that my comparison was far more accurate than I ever could have imagined. I just need to add this one observation:

Until my surgery, I simply assumed that severe medical crisis equated with high drama. With my heart about to stop beating, I figured my face should be turning purple as I fell to the floor, clutching my chest, pulling down at least one floor lamp in the process. Only then, should I pick up my phone.

Seventeen years before, I harbored a similar misconception regarding suicidal depression. Common sense told me that I should be on a window ledge looking down, someone 20 feet below looking up and leaning into yellow crime scene tape, trying to establish a rapport through a bullhorn.

The reality—both times for me—was far different. Over a period of more than two years, right to the very end, my depression convinced me it wasn't real. As my depression slowly claimed new territory, neuron by neuron, my mind came up with a million rationalizations. Call it a stealth condition. Even in the ER, demonstrably falling apart, I felt that I didn't belong there, that I was unworthy of medical attention.

The heart plays similar tricks. For nearly a year, whenever I exerted myself, my breathing would become labored. Over the months, even as my condition grew more apparent, I found reasons to avoid coming to the obvious conclusion. Even the day I called my brother, I wondered whether I wasn't being melodramatic.

My first hours in the ER seemed to confirm my hypochondria. My initial tests showed a robustly beating heart and fully oxygenated blood. To play it safe, the doctors decided to keep me overnight for further observation and testing. They lined up some routine stress tests for me the next day. Then a late blood test came in. An enzyme reaction indicated signs of my heart in distress. They would skip the stress tests and go straight to shoving a tiny camera up an artery.

Reading between the lines, I guessed the medical team would find a minor blockage, which they would rotor-rooter out. Then they would insert a supporting stent in the affected arterial region. Easy-peasy. I would be home a few hours after the procedure.

Instead, I woke up to holy fucking shit news. That evening, as I was getting out the word to those close to me, nurses and technicians prepped me for surgery to take place first thing in the morning. Talk about a stealth condition. The doctors and nurses and technicians, to a person, incidentally, congratulated me on my decision to go to the ER. My symptoms may have been subtle, they advised me, but the people who fail to get themselves to the ER are the ones they never get to hear about, the ones who don't live to tell their stories.

So, yes, a suicidal depression is like a heart attack. But I needed to experience both to fully appreciate the quiet perversity that is their MO. How they have a way of sneaking up on you in the dark, how they can deceive you into thinking it's all in your head, how they contrive to convince you that it will all blow over, that it's nothing, really, that you will wake up feeling much better, until—of course—you fail to wake up.

My return to life was nothing short of a major miracle. But before I could fully celebrate, my financial and living situation entirely collapsed. Meanwhile—and this is perfectly routine—over the next month, in a strange house, to go with the severe energy-depletion of my sternum mending and the rest of my body trying to figure out the new world order, I experienced a life-sucking major weight loss.

Oh, yes, and the type of draining depression that is part and parcel to patients recovering from heart surgery.

Welcome to a new form of death in life. At the same time, though, here I was, in deep gratitude, marveling at the miracle of my rebirth and resurrection, even while I was experiencing major obstacles with any task more complex than breathing.

But the important thing was—I was breathing. Real breaths, not labored breaths. Through the fog of my weakened condition, I began planning my life, the one that against all conceivable odds did not end months short of my sixty-seventh birthday.

As I write this, the weight is piling back on. My strength is returning. Once I am fully recovered—and this includes cataract surgery—I will be loading camping gear, a few didgeridoos, and other odds and ends into my car and taking to the road.

I'm calling it New Heart, New Start. I'm describing this new page of my life as a journey of discovery, healing, and connection. I plan on being on the road for 12 months.

I anticipate heading out in mid-December. The first stage of my journey will take me out of San Diego north to Joshua Tree National Park, then east to the natural wonders of Arizona, New Mexico, and lower Utah and Colorado. This leg of the trip will be devoted to my physical and spiritual healing. The land heals. The American Southwest is very generous in this regard.

Eventually—in the spring—I will find my way to New York City to be with my daughter and her family. Then up into New England before heading west across the northern states. From there, who knows?

All along the way, I am looking to make connections—both with people I have known over the years and with a new generation of boon companions. In the course of my travels, I anticipate a gradual falling away of my outer core, and a renewed relationship with my inner one. At many points along the way, I expect to be meeting myself for the first time. Such is our search for identity. I trust I will be happy with the outcome.

This book addressed the central question of why we seem to be born different, why we feel so out of place in a world that every day seems to offer yet more convincing proof that we were meant for life on any planet but this one. The original intention of this book had been far wider. Behavior, after all, is a limitless topic. But my return from heart surgery convinced me to keep a much tighter focus. Our search for identity cuts right to the heart of all our issues.

When I saw my cardiologist a week after being discharged, he asked me if I had any questions. "Only philosophical ones," I found myself answering. On the way home, I found myself contemplating the fact that here I was, all these years, still holding myself out to be an expert patient, the author of a bipolar expert series of books, no less. But expert patient, I began to realize, didn't begin to tell the whole story. Yes, I still identify as an expert patient, but the process of writing this book, together with the many personal realizations coming out of my heart surgery, had the effect of turning me into a philosopher-patient.

When I returned to these pages soon after the fog lifted, I began channeling that inner philosopher. Consciously, this was not the book I set out to write. Unconsciously, this was the book I needed to write.

Thank you for reading this. Until the next book in this series ...

STAY TUNED

MY NEXT book in this series will pick up where this one left off. That book will deal with recovery. To fill you in:

Recovery is a nonstarter without understanding. The first two books in this series, meant to be read together (in any order you wish), are devoted to acquiring a deep understanding into our moods and behavior. Once we are aware, for instance, that our moods are largely governed by our biological cycles and that our behavior has a lot to do with how we react to stress, and how the two influence the other, and how everything in turn is shaped by our personality traits, then our recovery strategies begin to fall into line.

Thus, proper sleep hygiene becomes central in getting a handle on our cycles. And learning to stop and smell the roses becomes one of many things we need to learn in nipping our stress response in the bud. And once we gain an insight into the personality deck that we have been dealt, we can begin playing our hand with a lot more skill.

That is only part of the picture. We will also learn to acquire some basic tools to navigate our often frightening social environment, such as how to carry on a conversation. Or things we need to consider in order to find a certain comfort within our own skins and meaning in our lives, such as cultivating an altruistic spirit. Or how to not take life so seriously for a change and just learn to be kids again.

Then there is the nitty gritty of smart lifestyle choices, such as diet and exercise and maintaining a healing home environment, along with the many things we need to learn, even if we don't choose to incorporate them into our daily routines such as meditation and yoga.

Plus getting out in nature and making music, which I used to regard as optional choices but I now consider absolutely essential. This is because our brains are wired to be immersed in both. Thanks to your already prior knowledge of how we are built to cycle in accord with the rhythms of nature, not to mention all your nerd knowledge of evolutionary psychology, this will be an easy sell.

And that's the point: If my next book were to be nothing more than lists of recovery tips and tricks, without the knowledge you gained in the first two books in this series I would be simply lecturing you. Try as I might otherwise, I would just be dispensing empty advice. My words would be going in one ear and out the other.

This is a good time to remind you once more that this is the second book in The Bipolar Expert Series. I am looking to have my next book out in 2016, and I need your help. You are my panel of experts.

Ever since I first began writing about bipolar, I have always regarded my efforts as a collaboration with my readers. Over the years, your wisdom and experience has guided me. You have been the source of my ideas, my mentors, my reality check, and the reason I get up in the morning.

Ordinarily, this is where I would ask you to follow me on Facebook and Twitter and go to my website and all the rest. But to make this work, you need to be on my mailing list. To this end, I have set up a special page on my new website. All you have to do is click on the link on this page and enter your email address in the form.

Again, you are my panel of experts. Please join me. Together, we can make a difference.

http://www.bipolarexpertseries.com/expertpanel1.html

ABOUT JOHN MCMANAMY

I AM an award-winning mental health writer and author, about to leave the San Diego area, my home for 10 years, to embark on a year-long cross-country tour. Where I will end up, who knows?

In 1999, soon after I was diagnosed with bipolar, I began researching and writing about my illness. This led to the 2006 publication of my book, *Living Well with Depression and Bipolar Disorder.* Frederick Goodwin, former head of the NIMH, called it "a vast trove of knowledge and insight." Nassir Ghaemi, now at Tufts, said "it breaks new ground." Susan Bergeson, then president of DBSA, called it "the perfect book for those living with mood disorders."

When not writing about bipolar, I enjoy getting out in nature and playing the didgeridoo.

Where to find me ...

McMan's Depression and Bipolar Web
www.mcmanweb.com

The Bipolar Expert Series (website):
www.bipolarexpertseries.com

The Bipolar Expert Series (blog):
http://blog.bipolarexpertseries.com

The Bipolar Expert Series (Facebook page):

https://www.facebook.com/bipolarexpertseries

@johnmcman (Twitter handle): https://twitter.com/johnmcman

And, once again, I ask you to join me on my panel of experts. Please copy the link below to sign up:
http://www.bipolarexpertseries.com/expertpanel1.html

READER PRAISE FOR MY FIRST BOOK IN THIS SERIES

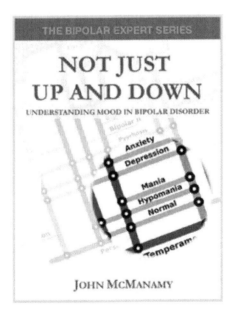

"JOHN is the perfect guide to help persons navigate the messy terrain of bipolar disorder ... All the chapters contain entertaining anecdotes, interesting studies, and sound advice, but I especially like what he had to say about normal, because going there is brave—what we know is extremely muddled, unclear, confusing. ... I appreciate his insights now because I am starting to reevaluate some of the beliefs I've held about my illness for 25 years. ... This is such a valuable book. John is ahead of his time in presenting balanced, well-researched information in a manner that is entertaining."—Therese Borchard

"He tears up the book, takes a look at the patient, and finds a new way to explain what is going on."—Willa Goodfellow.

"McManamy's commitment to people with mood disorders is well documented ... Walking the walk and not just talking the talk is the key to his expertise and ability to teach the 'average' person to become an expert patient."—Amy Peterson

"His way of thinking is original and creative, and his style of writing is compelling. ... He has a wealth of knowledge on mood disorders."— Bookworm57

"I tire of books that rehash information I already know and often tell depressing stories. Not Just Up and down is different!"—Whitney Best

"The takeaway message is the reader will be exposed to aspects of bipolar disorder that for me wouldn't have been discovered." Paul Cumming

"I thought I was pretty educated about this stuff, but this book is opening my eyes to so much that's new to me."—Snicky58

"John McManamy has the literary skills and knowledge far above nearly any bipolar author I have read in my lifetime."—HeyJude8

"His perspective is refreshing and thought-provoking. He has once again done a great service ..."—Carlos

"I loved the balance between research and personal anecdotes."—Jade Smith

"His thoughts on hypomania feeling the most 'normal,' on managing cycles within cycles, gives fascinating criticism to DSM-5 definitions that obscure rather than illuminate. He shows how mania and depression are not separate states but interlinked. Is hypomania a benign time or a prelude to a crash? It isn't the same for everyone. ... He has skin in the game." Herblady22

ABOUT THE BIPOLAR EXPERT SERIES

THE BIPOLAR Expert Series is a publishing project founded by John McManamy, author of *Living Well with Depression and Bipolar Disorder*. The project is aimed at helping you become your own expert patient, with six books covering every aspect of bipolar disorder.

These include (titles three through six are tentative) ...

NOT JUST UP AND DOWN, published Nov 2015, on our moods.

IN SEARCH OF OUR IDENTITY, published Nov 2016, on our behavior.

ARRIVING, scheduled for publication late 2017, on recovery.

Plus these three ...

YOUR BRAIN AND HOW TO USE IT, on what makes us tick, or not.

THESE MEDS AREN'T WORKING, scheduled for publication sometime in 2019, on what you need to do to make your treatments and therapies work for you.

I'M PERFECTLY SANE, YOU'RE THE ONE WITH THE PROBLEM, scheduled for publication in 2019), on bipolar relationships.

Again, please join my panel of experts:
http://www.bipolarexpertseries.com/expertpanel1.html

ACKNOWLEDGMENTS

THIS BOOK would not have been possible without the support and encouragement of a network of highly valued friends, not to mention some people I barely knew but who proved to be angels of mercy.

First, Louise Woo, a dear longtime friend and my mother confessor, who initially put the idea of self-publishing a series of bipolar books into my head, and kept encouraging me throughout.

Joanne Shortell, who advocates for the rights of those with service animals (she can help you at servicepoodle.com/contact-us). It was Joanne who got me started on this project. She came up with the titles for both The Bipolar Expert Series and the first book in the series, NOT JUST UP AND DOWN. In addition, she tipped me off to Scrivener's book-writing software, which spared me tons of time and frustration, plus she gave me some good pointers on marketing my work.

Maggie Reese, who I regard as a close friend, whose story I featured in my first book in this series, and who became my collaborator in our video series, *Bipolar Stuff in the Shack* with John and Maggie.

Kathryn Case, who generously offered to cast her eagle eye over my draft. She also stepped up in the same capacity with my first book in this series.

Leigha Cohen, who provided me with the space to make the necessary additions to this book while I was on the road.

Ana Rotta, who instinctively knew what I needed at just the right time.

Two people who rallied to my cause in the wake of my heart surgery include Jenefer Heartfire McCormick and Kelly Fitzpatrick. I could cite many others, but then I would incur the risk of leaving someone out.

Suffice to say, to know these two women is to have your faith in humanity restored. In particular, they provided tangible models for the principle of altruism, which I highlighted in my last chapter. It is an honor to dedicate this book to them.

Also, my brother James, who has the singular distinction of having driven me to the emergency room for two different conditions on two different coasts nearly two decades apart.

To Warner Recabaren, my local didge buddy and gracious host, who, together with his wife Karen, generously opened a place on his ranch to me.

Finally, to the medical team at Sharp Grossmont Hospital and their many partners, who performed a medical miracle on me. Nurses, by the way, are now my favorite people.

It wouldn't be right if I didn't pay tribute to my readers and those in the bipolar community—many who have followed and encouraged me since Day One. Perhaps you are one of them. But even if you came across me only today, you are a valued part of my tribe. For nearly two decades, you have not only given me a reason to wake up in the morning, but given me something to look forward to.

This brings me to Kevin Greim. He walked into our Princeton, NJ support group, a kid with a baseball cap on backward, goofy look on his face. We heard his story. It was the story of a sincere young man in a state of upheaval with nowhere to turn. The people in our group had a way of making him feel he had come to the right place. A rapport developed. He came back the next week. Then became a regular.

Kevin possessed a wisdom well beyond his years. In no time, he emerged as one of the group's leaders. Even people twice and three times his age sought out his wise counsel. At the same time, he was a bringer of joy. A fast friendship soon developed. Then my life turned upside down. There was a tearful farewell, then I was in California. One evening two years later, I arrived home to a chilling message on my answering machine: the morning before, he had taken his life. He was twenty-eight.

Life has no answers. But that doesn't stop us from searching for meaning. Who knows why we were put on earth, but if anyone asks I will say it's because of Kevin, my good friend. Nothing more to say ...

NOTES

THIS SPACE is for sources that didn't receive adequate recognition in the main text, and for various sundry asides.

CHAPTERS ONE AND TWO

My personal story is illustrative of how an underlying personality trait can affect various mood states. In the old days, these types of personal accounts would have been featured as "case studies" in leading medical journals. Now, they tend to be dismissed as "anecdotal." In my first book in this series, I cited numerous authorities who lamented the loss of what I call the "observational wisdom" gained from paying close attention to patients.

This book contains no shortage of examples of the knowledge we have acquired from a host of scientific disciplines. But too often, in their quest for hard data, scientists lose track of who they are actually studying.

This leads to making simplistic assumptions, which in turn leads to asking the wrong questions in pursuit of irrelevant answers.

These days, with the devaluing of careful clinical observation, patients themselves represent the best source of observational wisdom. Scientists and clinicians, unfortunately, suffer a huge deficit in accepting this reality.

CHAPTER THREE

It is no accident that Robert Sapolsky is featured across the chapters in Parts Two and Four. He is one of those rare scientists who recognizes the limits to thinking inside of specialized "buckets." Take it from a neuro guy who studies baboons in the wild: What makes sense according to the dictates of one specialty may be insupportable according to the conventions of another.

An example of Sapolsky's approach: If you're investigating behavior at the neurotransmitter level, you need to step back and find out what was going on an hour or two before that particular behavior took place—say with how your immediate environment affected hormonal production, which in turn may have predisposed you to act in a certain way. Then step back further to earlier times in your life, then to fetal development, genes, and so on, back to evolution.

This is set out in the introductory lecture to a 2010 human behavioral biology course he presented at Stanford, and available for viewing on the university's website. I trust I have adopted the spirit of this wide bandwidth of inquiry by attempting to harmonize genes-cells-circuits with evolutionary biology.

Incidentally, bipolar has to be the most hermetic of all major fields in psychiatry, an often ridiculous bucket inside a bucket. To oversimplify: The academic bipolar establishment fails to offer a coherent view of bipolar, much less integrate what they know into the broad universe of human behavior. There is a small enlightened group who do bring coherency to their specialty, who I extensively relied on in my first book in this series. The catch: These particular experts take a dim view of the specialists in the next bucket over, ones who operate in the field of personality disorders. Oy!

Sapolsky, "A Gene for Nothing," Oct 1, 1997 *Discover Magazine.*

Some observations on the studies I cite in this book:

It is all too easy to cherrypick behavior studies to fit a narrative we are trying to build. The result can be as misleading as making things up. A short list of research study problems include methodological flaws, exaggeration of the results, burying inconvenient findings, generalizing a specific finding in support of a suspect general principle, and lack of replication.

Add to that what may happen when the popular press gets hold of a study, and we have another layer of distortion. This is true even with honest and accurate reporting.

214

Then there are those of us (I include myself, here) who seek to connect disparate dots into a coherent narrative. This raises a whole new set of problems, especially if we happen to become over-invested in our own narratives.

In brief, my methodology, as such:

The studies I cite in this book either tend to be landmark studies—ones that opened up new fields of inquiry—or fit solidly inside a well-established line of inquiry from more than one field, or are supported by a host of similar studies. Ideally, any cited study meets all three criteria.

Having said that, with human behavior we quickly venture into large tracts of scientific Terra Incognita.

Thus, rather than close down the conversation for lack of hard data, it is appropriate to make speculative leaps, but we need to use as a spring board a strong body of evidence from areas we have succeeded in charting. Moreover, these leaps need to be red-flagged.

Hopefully, we all wind up more informed, with our eyes opened wider than before. That's my intention, anyway. Now for some study citations:

Caspi et al, "Influence of life stress on depression: moderation by a polymorphism in the 5-HTT gene," *Science*, July 18, 2003.

Hariri et al, "Serotonin transporter genetic variation and the response of the human amygdala," *Science*, July 19, 2002.

In 2003, *Science* cited the above two studies, along with others, as the second-biggest scientific breakthrough of the year. Years later, scientists may still engage in food fights over the findings of the Caspi study in particular, but there is no denying its impact on how it has clarified our understanding of nature-nurture and of genes and environment interacting with each other to influence behavior.

Sapolsky, "Gene therapy for psychiatric disorders," Feb, 2003 *Am J Psychiatry.*

The term, "chronically normal," comes from the legendary mental health advocate, Fred Frese.

CHAPTER FOUR

Re evolutionary "theory," there is nothing "theoretical" about evolution. In science, a theory is understood to provide a coherent explanation of an underlying reality, typically employing general principles to predict specific occurrences.

Dawkins, *The Selfish Gene: 40th Anniversary Edition*, OUP, 2016.

Curry, "Archaeology: The Milk Revolution," July 31, 2003 *Nature*.

CHAPTER FIVE

Kandel, 2000 *Nobel Biography*.

Kandel, "The Molecular Biology of Memory Storage: A Dialogue between Genes and Synapses," *Nobel Lecture*, Dec 8, 2000.

CHAPTER SIX

One of the things holding back bipolar research, incidentally, is lack of a "rat model" for bipolar. We can torture rats, for instance into a state of learned helplessness that mimics depression, and we can inject the same creatures with methamphetamines to induce a state that bears a semblance to mania or psychosis, but that is not the same as getting the animal to cycle up and down.

Churakov et al, "Rodent Evolution: Back to the Root," *Molecular Biology and Evolution*, OUP, 2010

Probably the most cited stress-rodent study:
Weaver et al, "Epigenetic programming by maternal behavior," June 27, 2004 *Nature Neuroscience*.

Northoff, "Psychoanalysis and the Brain – Why Did Freud Abandon Neuroscience?" April 2, 2012 *Front Psychol*.

Re the early DSMs: The first book in this series, NOT JUST UP AND DOWN, contains a detailed account of the development of psychiatry's diagnostic bible, the DSM. My quick take: Basically, the early DSMs I and

II are not the Freudian rubbish that modern commentators have made them out to be. At the same time, the "modern" DSMs III, III-R, IV, and 5 are at best rough guides and at worst totally misleading.

CHAPTER SEVEN

My account here—as well as accounts in later chapters concerning our evolutionary development—is necessarily over-simplistic. It may be, for instance, that Lucy was perfectly capable of crafting stone tools, but this book is hardly the place to go into all that.

Callaway, "Human brain shaped by duplicate genes," May 3 *Nature News*.

For Dr Manji's analysis, I drew upon my notes from personal interviews, lectures at conferences, slide presentations, and journal articles too numerous to single out. Back when he was at the NIMH (to about 2010), I would make a regular habit of entering his name into *PubMed* searches. In this way, I never ran out of nerd-geek brain science stuff to write about.

Shenk, "What Makes Us Happy?" June 2009 *Atlantic*.

Waldinger, "What Makes a Good Life?" *TEDx Beacon Street*, Nov 2015.

CHAPTER EIGHT

In various chapters throughout this book, I make use of reader polls and surveys, plus reader feedback. These are hardly on the same level of authority as scientific studies, but they do yield intriguing insights. The reason we don't see this type of information turning up in scientific studies has to do with the byzantine processes in obtaining grants and jumping through publishing hoops, a process that may involve years. My approach: Just ask some questions online and post your results.

CHAPTER NINE

This is but one of two mentions of Emil Kraepelin in this book. By contrast, Kraepelin was at the root of just about everything I touched on in my first book in this series.

CHAPTER TEN

The child poverty study was cited by Robert Sapolsky in his online Stanford course (see notes to Chapter Three).

Heim et al, "Pituitary-adrenal and autonomic responses to stress in women after sexual and physical abuse in childhood,"Aug 2, 2000 *JAMA*.

CHAPTER ELEVEN

Strakowski et al, "A preliminary FMRI study of sustained attention in euthymic, unmedicated bipolar disorder," Sept, 2004 *Neuropsychopharmacology*.

For an excellent account of adult ADD, written from the perspective of someone married to an ADD partner, check out Gina Pera's *Is It You or Me or Adult ADD*, 1201 Alarm Press, 2008.

For a study on how multitasking interferes with memory:
Capp et al, "Deficit in switching between functional brain networks underlies the impact of multitasking on working memory in older adults," April 26, 2011 *Proc Natl Acad Sci*. The "refrigerator moment" metaphor, is attributable one of the study's coauthors, Adam Gazzaley of UCSF.

CHAPTER TWELVE

For a 40-year perspective of the marshmallow study by the original author, see: Mischel et al, "'Willpower' over the life span: decomposing self-regulation," April, 2011 *Soc Cogn Affect Neurosci*.

For the brain scan follow-up to the marshmallow study, see: Casey et al, "Behavioral and neural correlates of delay of gratification 40 years later," Sept 6, 2011, *Proc Natl Acad Sci*.

My commentary on how pleasure/reward affects bipolar is based on the following review article: Alloy et al, "Role of Reward Sensitivity and Processing in Major Depressive and Bipolar Spectrum Disorders," Sept, 2016 *Behav Ther.*

Risk-taking is associated with novelty-seeking. A lot of attention has been given to the "novelty-seeking" gene variation, DRD4-7, that codes the dopamine-4 receptor. The idea, popularized in Peter Whybrow's 2006 book, *American Mania: When More is Not Enough*, was that those deficient in dopamine tend to seek out risky and self-destructive thrills. The proposition is entirely valid. It's just that the weight of the study evidence indicates we may be barking up the wrong gene variation.

For the study on how pleasure affects our political thinking:
Westen et al, "Neural Bases of Motivated Reasoning: An fMRI Study of Emotional Constraints on Partisan Political Judgment in the 2004 U.S. Presidential Election", Nov 2016 *J Cogn Neurosci.*

The obsession aspect of romantic attraction comes from Helen Fischer of Rutgers University. I heard her talk about the biology of love and lust at the 2004 American Psychiatric Association annual meeting in New York.

My account of the biology of OCD is based on a talk that Neal Swerdlow of UCSD presented to NAMI San Diego in 2009.

CHAPTER THIRTEEN

Inevitably, commentaries on borderline personality disorder tend to be written to help protect the innocent bystander. This stands in complete contrast to just about all of the bipolar literature, which views the patient sympathetically. One example of the former, which is actually an excellent book:
Mason and Kreger, *Stop Walking on Eggshells: Taking Your Life Back When Someone You Care About Has Borderline Personality Disorder*, 2nd edition, New Harbinger, 2010.
More recent books and articles on borderline are devoted to seeing things from the patient's perspective, but my point remains.

My cursory scan of the narcissist literature also reveals a similar point of view, aimed at the victim, never the patient. Since the classic narcissist, of course, would be the last to admit he needs help, writing a self-help book would be an exercise in personal futility and economic folly.

No discussion of narcissism would be complete without bringing Donald Trump into the conversation. Not only does he easily fit the diagnostic criteria for narcissism, but, according to Johns Hopkins psychologist John Gartner he falls into a particularly execrable strain known as "malignant narcissim," a type of narcissist with a generous portion of sociopathy.

Dr Gartner has succeeded in rallying tens of thousands of his colleagues in mental health under the rubric of "Duty to Warn," whose premise is that psychiatrists and psychologists need to make the public aware of the clear and present danger that a demonstrably mentally unstable President such as Donald Trump poses. On its Facebook page, Dr Gartner has posted numerous articles, including his own. The most insightful one to date is by psychoanalyst Michael Bader, "Psychoanalyzing Donald Trump," published June 3, 2017 in *The National Memo*.

At the time of adding this note (June, 2017), Mr Trump is under federal investigation for obstruction of justice.

For an excellent historical perspective on histrionic:
Novartis et al, "Historical Roots of Histrionic Personality Disorder," Sept 25, 2015 Frontiers in Psychology.

For a quick take on Zsa Zsa Gabor, check out this Dec 18, 2016 *LA Times* obituary: "Zsa Zsa Gabor dies at 99; she had glamour and husbands in spades."

CHAPTER FOURTEEN

Dunning and Kruger, "Unskilled and unaware of it: how difficulties in recognizing one's own incompetence lead to inflated self-assessments. *Dec*, 1999 *J Pers Soc Psychol*.

Paul Piff explains his Monopoly Game study in a 2013 *TED Talk*, "Does Money Make You Mean?" The study, together with others he has conducted, is more concerned with how wealth and privilege influence people's lack of regard for others. But it also serves as a strong object lesson for how easy it is to spectacularly delude ourselves into overestimating our own abilities.

For an explanation of the depressive realism model of depression, check out Nassir Ghaemi's article: "Feeling and Time: The Phenomenology of Mood Disorders, Depressive Realism, and Existential Psychotherapy," Jan, 2007 *Schizophr Bull.*
My first book in this series relied heavily on Dr Ghaemi's work.

CHAPTER FIFTEEN

Regier et al, "Comorbidity of mental disorders with alcohol and other drug abuse. Results from the Epidemiologic Catchment Area (ECA) Study," Nov, 1990 *JAMA.*

Banerjee, "Neurotransmitters in alcoholism: A review of neurobiological and genetic studies," Jan-Mar, 2014 *Indian J Hum Genet.*

Volkow et al, "Caffeine increases striatal dopamine D2/D3 receptor availability in the human brain," April, 2015 *Transl Psychiatry.*

Re long-distance running: I ran track and cross-country in high school, but was not motivated to pursue it after that. But my long-ago involvement has kept my interest intact.

Dubreucq et al, "Ventral tegmental area cannabinoid type-1 receptors control voluntary exercise performance," May, 2013 *Biol Psychiatry.* 2013.

Lavelle, "New Brain Effects behind 'Runner's High,'" Oct 8, 2015 *Chemical & Engineering News,* republished in SciAm.

Alexander et al, "The effect of housing and gender on morphine self-administration in rats," July, 1978 Psychopharmacology (Berl).

Hari, "The Likely Cause of Addiction Has Been Discovered, and It Is Not What You Think," Jan 20, 2015 *HuffPo.*

CHAPTER SIXTEEN

For an excellent insight into why "normal" is not necessarily desirable, check out Rosie King's 2014 TEDMed Talk, "How Autism Freed Me to Be Myself."

CHAPTER SEVENTEEN

Buddhist teachings notably emphasize the futility of clinging to one's precious ego, with its attendant delusions. The principle is on ample display in other faith and spiritual traditions, as well. In a business context, we hear the conversation in relation to those who lead their companies into financial disaster. Old ways of thinking quickly become delusional in shifting markets or volatile financial times. Different worlds, same lessons.

CHAPTER EIGHTEEN

For the sake of simplicity, I have applied Erectus in the broad sense of including Ergaster, Rudolfensis, and Heidlebergensis and other varieties of Homo. This simplication has wide anthropological support. In the narrow sense, Erectus relates only to those who left their fossils in certain parts of eastern Asia. Thus, "Java Man" and "Peking Man."

Recent findings of Neanderthal and Denisovan DNA turning up in our genome have complicated the out of Africa narrative, but hardly overturned it. Clearly, anthropologists and geneticists will come up with other findings that will add further layers of complexity to the picture. But these learned discussions should not distract us from our main story line.

Florio, "Human-specific gene ARHGAP11B promotes basal progenitor amplification and neocortex expansion," Feb 26, 2015 *Science*.

Boyd, "Human-Chimpanzee Differences in a FZD8 Enhancer Alter Cell-Cycle Dynamics in the Developing Neocortex," February 19, 2015 Current Biology.

Teffer and Semendeferi, "Human prefrontal cortex: Evolution, development, and pathology," *Progress in Brain Research*, Vol. 195, Elsevier, 2012.

Rather than cite a zillion books and journal articles on why our thinking is not all that rational, I simply refer you to Jonah Lehrer's 2009 Book, *How We Decide*, Daniel Kahneman's *Thinking, Fast and Slow (2011)*, and Chabris et al's *The Invisible Gorilla* (Crown, 2006).

Christopher Mooney's *The Republican Brain (2012)*, drawing heavily upon the work of psychologist Jonathan Haidt of New York University, details the many reasons our brains are ill-equipped to make rational decisions at the voting booth, with the fate of the world resting in our hands.

Mooney maintains that Republicans are particularly bad at this. In light of the surprise 2016 Presidential results, I would contend that Democrats, for different reasons, live in their own hopeless fantasy world. My take, for whatever it is worth: Republicans stupidly vote for policies palpably harmful to just about everyone while Democrats stupidly can't imagine anyone being stupid enough to vote that way.

The key issue here is that to change your thinking, whether liberal or conservative, you are fighting against your basic personality traits. This is why changing other people's minds is futile.

CHAPTER NINETEEN

Rogers et al, "Advantages of having a lateralized brain," Dec 7, 2004 *Proc Biol Sci*.

Re the "bollocks" comment. From my first book in this series:
How bad was it? At a 2011 NAMI CA convention in Sacramento, Cameron Carter of UC Davis told a story of how as a student in the UK back in the late seventies, he came across a library journal article, hot off the press, that contained the first brain scan evidence of a biological link to schizophrenia. "Bollocks!" someone had scribbled on the page.

Parker, "Asymmetrical brain gives up its secrets," Jan15, 2009 *Sci GoGo*.

Carey, "Beyond DNA: Epigenetics," *Natural History*, 2012.

Heijmansa, "Persistent epigenetic differences associated with prenatal exposure to famine in humans," Nov 4, 2008 *Proc Natl Acad Sci.*

Our main suspect candidate for a worldwide natural disaster that nearly wiped out the human race concerns a super volcano that erupted 75,000 years ago in what is now Lake Toba in Sumatra. The eruption was 100 times larger than the largest eruption of modern times, an 1815 blast from Mt Tambora in Indonesia. That eruption caused "the year without a summer" in the northern hemisphere in 1816. The Toba eruption, many believe, would have plunged the world into a volcanic winter, leaving only small and isolated human populations behind.

This theory suffered a major setback in 2013 when a research team from Oxford University failed to find supporting geological evidence from core samples from Lake Malawi in East Africa, near ground zero for our earliest Sapien fossil remains.

Nevertheless, it is widely acknowledged that during this time, the Sapien population was down to endangered species levels, to perhaps as low as 3,000 breeding pairs. Never mind the super volcano—Eve's descendants were clearly having trouble adapting to the usual suite of ordinary disasters Mother Nature happened to throw their way.

CHAPTER TWENTY

McAuliffe, "If Modern Humans Are So Smart, Why Are Our Brains Shrinking," Jan 20, 2011, *Discover.*

Hadaway, "The effect of housing and gender on preference for morphine-sucrose solutions in rats," 1979 *Psychopharmacology.* The study is still a matter of hot debate in addiction circles, but when combined with endless studies comparing rodents living in enriched vs impoverished environments, we begin to appreciate what the lack of a stimulating environment may do to humans.

As for why we're not wired to "think," I refer you to Lehrer, Kahneman et all cited in the notes to Chapter Eighteen.

CHAPTER TWENTY-ONE

Barbara Oakley's 2007 book, *Evil Genes*, explains altruism vs opportunism as a sort of evolutionary arms race, where one side or the other gains temporary advantage until equilibrium is eventually restored, whereupon the cycle starts up anew. For instance, opportunists find altruists easy prey. But if they're too successful, they no longer have prey to feed on. We're using the term, altruism, loosely here. Meanwhile, by virtue of their ability to cooperate and form alliances, altruists have their own evolutionary advantages—until, of course, the opportunists come up with new ways of outsmarting them. On and on it goes. Dr Oakley argues that the development of agriculture opened a new niche for the opportunist. From there, it is easy to advance our own arguments on how the opportunists exploited their new advantage to devastating effect.

For a layperson's explanation on tit for tat: Kay, "Generous Tit for Tat: A Winning Strategy," Dec 19, 2011 *Forbes*.

Two popular books that offer an excellent sense of the brutal growing pains from a hunter-gatherer society to an agricultural and urban one include Karen Armstrong's *Fields of Blood: Religion and the History of Violence* (2014) and Yuval Harari's *Sapiens: A Brief History of Mankind* (2015).

In addition, I must credit Dr Harari's book as inspiration for my decision to organize Parts Two and Four as a four billion-year history of humankind. In understanding the now, it is essential that we know where we came from and where we may be heading.

The field of evolutionary psychology is infinitely more complex than what I describe here, and embraces related fields such as anthropology and studies into animal behavior. Leading lights in the field of evolutionary psychology include Charles Darwin, who started it all, plus Leda Cosmides and John Tooby of UC Santa Barbara, who offer an excellent online intro, "Evolutionary Psychology: A Primer."

Randolf Nesse of the University of Arizona State offers excellent psychiatric insights into why conditions such as depression and anxiety offered sufficient adaptive advantages for their genes to have been passed down from generation to generation. I heard Dr Nesse deliver a featured lecture at the 2005 American Psychiatric Association in Atlanta. I took careful notes.

Black box warning: Evolutionary psychology offers excellent insights into how we evolved behaving as we do. Moreover, it is anchored solidly in evolutionary science. Nevertheless, we need to be mindful of the fact that it deals mainly in speculation rather than hard evidence. We are only imagining what may have been going through a distant ancestor's mind at an ancient watering hole. We weren't actually there, observing and taking notes.

I'm sure the idea that we were bred to be compliant has to be a well-established one, but thus far I have failed to come up an account that I can acknowledge. I will incorporate any acknowledgement into my next update of this book.

One notorious study—the Milgram Experiment—sheds invaluable light on our apparent willingness to follow orders rather than question authority. In the experiment, researchers at Yale ordered test subjects to inflict harm on fellow subjects. Surprisingly, most of the subjects did as they were told. Follow-up indicated that the subjects were influenced by the researchers' positions of authority.

The study has been widely attacked on many levels, from ethical to methodological. Nevertheless, there can be no intelligent conversation on why people are so willing to do as they are told without reference to this study.

The citation for the Milgram Experiment: Milgram, "Behavioral Study of Obedience," Oct 1963 *Journal of Abnormal and Social Psychology.*

Another equally notorious study on authority is the "Stanford Prison Experiment," where one group of students proved all too eager in stepping into their assigned roles as prison guards while the other group proved all too compliant as prisoners. The study was published in a naval research review in 1973.

CHAPTER TWENTY-TWO

For the Mediterranean Dark Ages and the Golden Age of Classical Greece, respectively:

Eric Cline's *1177 BC: The Year Civilization Collapsed*, (2014).
Thomas Cahill's *Sailing the Wine-Dark Sea: Why the Greeks Matter*, (2004).

Arrian of Nicodemus wrote of Alexander's campaigns four centuries after he died, so we have to take the speech with a grain of salt. What makes this account believable, though, is that Arrian's seven-volume history otherwise comes across as a hagiography. Apparently, public displays of extreme sociopathy add a glow to any conqueror's halo.

It is always a risky undertaking trying to assign various psychiatric diagnoses to historical figures. But in the case of ancient conquerors born into privilege who treat people horribly for their own self-aggrandizement while claiming to be the son of the a god, hitting upon sociopath and narcissist was not much of a stretch.

This particular Cluster B combo plate can also be described as a "malignant narcissist," and may apply to a current President of the US, as well, but we won't mention names.

CHAPTER TWENTY-THREE

Wikipedia offers an excellent bio on John von Neumann and his achievements.

CHAPTER TWENTY-FOUR

I've heard others refer to nonlinear thinking in their everyday speech. What I describe here represents my own idiosyncratic take.

CHAPTER TWENTY-FIVE

Marano, "Trusting Intuition," May 4, 2004 *Psychology Today*.

The firefighter and art expert examples receive the full treatment in Malcolm Gladwell's *Blink: The Power of Thinking without Thinking* (2007).

I'm deeply indebted to Scott Barry Kaufman for his insights into the schizotypal-creativity connection, in particular his Oct 3, 2013 post on his

Beautiful Minds blog on *Scientific American*: "The Real Link Between Creativity and Mental Illness."

Kaufman, "On the interrelation between reduced lateralization, schizotypy, and creativity," Jul 28 2014 *Front Psychol.*

Fink, "Creativity and schizotypy from the neuroscience perspective," 2013 *Cogn Affect Behav Neurosci.*

Murray et al, "The clinical significance of creativity in bipolar disorder," *Clin Psychol Rev.*

Carson, "Creativity and Psychopathology: A Shared Vulnerability Model." 2011 *Can J Psychiatry.*

CHAPTER TWENTY-SIX

Most of us know of the bipolar-creativity connection through Kay Jamison's *Touched By Fire* (1996). The book features a short list of creative bipolars such as Van Gough and Lord Byron, plus various long lists of poets and classical composers and such.

CHAPTER TWENTY-SEVEN

Carhart-Harris et al, "The entropic brain: a theory of conscious states informed by neuroimaging research with psychedelic drugs," February 3, 2014 *Front. Hum. Neurosci.*

Danzico, "Brains of Buddhist monks scanned in meditation study," April 24, 2011 *BBC News.*

CHAPTER TWENTY-EIGHT

Someone shoot me. I simply can't believe I wrote an account even remotely sympathetic of Richard Nixon.

CHAPTER TWENTY-NINE

Altruism will be a major theme in my next book in this series, on recovery.

FINALLY

IF YOU actually read through my notes, then I know—totally know—that you are a dedicated follower. Let's stay in touch. First, more books are in the pipeline, not to mention articles and blog posts. This means I can use your help in shaping my ideas and in getting the word out.

Once again, where to find me ...

The Bipolar Expert Series (website):
www.bipolarexpertseries.com

The Bipolar Expert Series (blog):
http://blog.bipolarexpertseries.com
The Bipolar Expert Series (Facebook page):
https://www.facebook.com/bipolarexpertseries

@johnmcman (Twitter handle):
https://twitter.com/johnmcman

But most important, I need you to join my panel of experts. My next book is all about you, and you are the true expert. We need to have a two-way conversation. These conversations will shape my next book. Together, we can make a difference. Here's the link to my sign-up page. Talk soon ...
    http://www.bipolarexpertseries.com/expertpanel1.html

51062911R00128

Made in the USA
Middletown, DE
07 November 2017